T0271401

Markets vs Public Health Systems

Problems related to the functioning of public healthcare systems encourage the search for alternative solutions, for example to ensure improved access to medical services. However, these proposals also require appropriate theoretical support to better present and apply them. This book draws on Austrian Economics to provide a theoretical framework to support greater involvement of the private sector to improve inefficiencies in public healthcare.

The Austrian School of Economics has a solid theoretical output describing and explaining the functioning of many aspects of the market economy (e.g. money, prices, interest rate, or capital). This work applies those principles to a market-based healthcare system and its individual elements, including health insurance. The study in these chapters is divided into two parts. The first part contains the theoretical aspects of the functioning of a complete market system. Particular importance is placed on presenting health insurance as a market institution and exploring its role in the market system. This examination also includes an analysis of alternative forms of financing access to medical services, such as direct payments, medical savings accounts, medical subscriptions, and charity. Additionally, solid counterarguments are provided for so-called market failures: asymmetric information, public goods, and monopolies. The second part of the book explores the theoretical aspects of interventionism and the functioning of public systems, and aims to better highlight the sources of the associated problems.

This work provides an important contribution to the literature on health economics, healthcare management and policy, and Austrian Economics more broadly. It is essential reading for health economists and those holding key public positions related to healthcare.

Łukasz Jasiński is an economist and researcher at the Faculty of Economics of the Maria Curie-Sklodowska University (Poland, Lublin).

"Łukasz Jasiński explains flawed public health systems and presents the merits of a genuine market approach. A major innovation is his elaboration of health insurance from an Austrian School perspective."
– **Robert P. Murphy**, economist and co-author of *The Primal Prescription: Surviving the "Sick Care" Sinkhole*

Routledge Focus on Economics and Finance

The fields of economics are constantly expanding and evolving. This growth presents challenges for readers trying to keep up with the latest important insights. Routledge Focus on Economics and Finance presents short books on the latest big topics, linking in with the most cutting-edge economics research.

Individually, each title in the series provides coverage of a key academic topic, whilst collectively the series forms a comprehensive collection across the whole spectrum of economics.

Islamic Economics and COVID-19
The Economic, Social and Scientific Consequences of a Global Pandemic
Masudul Alam Choudhury

The Economics of Intellectual Property and Openness
The Tragedy of Intangible Abundance
Bartłomiej Biga

Economics, Education and Youth Entrepreneurship
International Perspectives
Marian Noga and Andrzej Brzeziński

Markets vs Public Health Systems
Perspectives from the Austrian School of Economics
Łukasz Jasiński

For more information about this series, please visit: www.routledge.com/Routledge-Focus-on-Economics-and-Finance/book-series/RFEF

Markets vs Public Health Systems

Perspectives from the Austrian School of Economics

Łukasz Jasiński

Routledge
Taylor & Francis Group

LONDON AND NEW YORK

First published 2022
by Routledge
4 Park Square, Milton Park, Abingdon, Oxon OX14 4RN

and by Routledge
605 Third Avenue, New York, NY 10158

Routledge is an imprint of the Taylor & Francis Group, an informa business

© 2022 Łukasz Jasiński

The right of Łukasz Jasiński to be identified as author of this work has been asserted in accordance with sections 77 and 78 of the Copyright, Designs and Patents Act 1988.

All rights reserved. No part of this book may be reprinted or reproduced or utilised in any form or by any electronic, mechanical, or other means, now known or hereafter invented, including photocopying and recording, or in any information storage or retrieval system, without permission in writing from the publishers.

Trademark notice: Product or corporate names may be trademarks or registered trademarks, and are used only for identification and explanation without intent to infringe.

British Library Cataloguing-in-Publication Data
A catalogue record for this book is available from the British Library

Library of Congress Cataloging-in-Publication Data
Names: Jasiński, Łukasz, author.
Title: Markets vs public health systems : perspectives from the Austrian School of Economics / Łukasz Jasiński.
Description: Milton Park, Abingdon, Oxon ; New York, NY : Routledge, 2022. |
Series: Routledge focus on economics and finance |
Includes bibliographical references and index.
Identifiers: LCCN 2021041215 (print) |
LCCN 2021041216 (ebook) | ISBN 9781032193939 (hardback) |
ISBN 9781032193946 (paperback) | ISBN 9781003258957 (ebook)
Subjects: LCSH: Public health--Austria. | Health care reform--Economic aspects. | Health insurance--Economic aspects.
Classification: LCC RA493 .J37 2022 (print) |
LCC RA493 (ebook) | DDC 368.38/2009436--dc23/eng/20211007
LC record available at https://lccn.loc.gov/2021041215
LC ebook record available at https://lccn.loc.gov/2021041216

ISBN: 978-1-032-19393-9 (hbk)
ISBN: 978-1-032-19394-6 (pbk)
ISBN: 978-1-003-25895-7 (ebk)

DOI: 10.4324/9781003258957

Typeset in Times New Roman
by Taylor & Francis Books

To Epaminondas: First Among the Greeks

Contents

About the author

Łukasz Jasiński is an economist and researcher at the Faculty of Economics of the Maria Curie-Sklodowska University (Poland, Lublin). In 2021, he completed his doctoral dissertation entitled 'Market processes and interventionism in the health system of the United States of America from the view of the Austrian School of Economics'.

He is also a regular collaborator and lecturer at the Mises Institute (Poland, Wroclaw), where he publishes his original series of essays entitled: 'On the way to the market health system'.

In 2016, he won the fourth edition of the 'Ethics in Finance: The Robin Cosgrove Award' (2016 – Polish edition). His essay, titled 'Ethics in life insurance', earned first place in the competition, which is organized annually by the Polish Bank Association and Banking Ethics Committee. More information is available here: https://www.researchga te.net/publication/327498403_Ethics_in_Life_Insurance.

About the author

Introduction

This book is a theoretical introduction to my future publications on healthcare, especially the relationships between interventionism and market processes and their impact on access to medical services (e.g. in the US). These issues were presented in terms of the Austrian School of Economics, which has considerable theoretical achievements devoted to the analysis of the market economy and interventionism.

The two parts of this book deal with the theoretical aspects of market and interventionist solutions in the area of health systems, which aims to create appropriate arguments for the former. At the same time, creating a theoretical framework for the functioning of the market health system and constructive criticism of the so-called market failures are the main goals of this book. This is to help promote stronger market solutions in this area.

Nowadays, the provision and financing of rare medical goods and services takes place mainly through public systems, and the share of the market or private initiatives in this area is quite limited – both in financial and regulatory terms.

However, after many decades of experience in the development of public health systems, there are still no uniform solutions in this area, and the problems encountered by public systems existing in different countries are the reason for seeking alternative forms of organizing healthcare systems. The negative effects related to the domination of the public healthcare system (e.g. rising costs and expenses or lengthening queues for benefits) in many countries contribute to the fact that widely discussed ideas in this area include, among others: increasing the role of private health insurance as forms of financing access to medical services, decentralization of the institutional structure responsible for financing access, and the provision of medical services, giving more freedom to the consumer in choosing suppliers of such services or adding elements limiting the moral hazard and increasing costs to a given system (e.g. co-payment).

DOI: 10.4324/9781003258957-1

The above changes are also intended to help better adapt public systems to increasingly important challenges or problems: negative demographic trends, the increasing number of chronic diseases, or costly technological changes.

From the perspective of the Austrian School, however, it can be said that these systems are part of a hampered market economy where the government interferes with the economy (including the health system) through commands and prohibitions. In this context, the problem of interventionism, according to representatives of this school, is not the difficulty of determining 'natural', 'fair', or 'appropriate' tasks of the state and government, as these may change over time depending on conditions. From an economic point of view, this problem boils down to the question of how the interventionist system works. Can it achieve the goals that its adherents have set for themselves? This question has its own specific connotation in terms of the organization of health systems.

However, public health systems do not have to be one solution. An alternative to them may be a system entirely based on market solutions. In this case, however, theoretical arguments in its favour should be properly presented – which is one of the goals of this study.

Contrary to public solutions, the market system does not have a 'rigid' or formalized structure. It is also subject to certain dynamic changes caused, among others, by the processes of competition between suppliers or insurers, etc. Very often there are also accusations that the poor or the sick would not be financially able to afford treatment with the simultaneous inability to take advantage of health insurance. At the same time, it is supposed to prove that market solutions are faulty.

In order to adequately counter these objections, first of all, one should look at individual (main) elements of the market system, namely private sources of financing access to medical services: medical insurance, medical subscriptions, direct payments, and charity support. This will allow a better understanding of how it works.

Particular attention was paid in particular to insurance institution. In the spirit of the Austrian School, insurance is a market institution that arises and evolves thanks to unrestricted market processes, such as, for example, money. Insurance does not have to be the most popular option for such a system to function efficiently. At the same time, the institution has certain limitations (but which should not be seen as disadvantages) that make alternative solutions necessary. Interestingly, the subject of insurance or insurance markets was not particularly developed in this paradigm. The subject of insurance (economic and social) appears, for example, in L. von Mises (1998, pp. 833–834) or M. N. Rothbard (2006, pp. 74–77, 127–133), but these are only short fragments that can be further elaborated.

In the context of the discussed issues, it will be particularly helpful to use the achievements of the Austrian School of Economics. Thanks to the appropriate reference to the issue of probability, risk, or the role of economic calculation, it will be possible to adequately and exhaustively reflect the essence of health insurance and (in a broader context) of the market health system. In this case, an appropriate (i.e. rational) structure of financing access to medical services without the imposed domination of insurance is of particular importance.

Appropriate arguments showing the superiority of market solutions must also refer to the most frequently raised market failures: asymmetric information, the possibility of providing public goods, and the issue of monopolies. The above issues constitute the first part of the work.

The second part presents theoretical aspects of interventionism and its impact on the processes forming the market health system. It will also be important to present the principles of operation of the public system. As a result, they will be easier to compare with the market system. The use of the term 'health system' instead of the commonly used term 'healthcare system' is also adequately justified.

References

Mises L., 1998, *Human action. A treatise on economics*, Auburn: Ludwig von Mises Institute.

Rothbard M. N., 2006, *Making economic sense*, Auburn: Ludwig von Mises Institute.

Part I

Market processes in the health system

Introduction

Arguments in favour of market solutions in the health system of any country in the first place must be based on correct theoretical inference, which will be able to adequately show the specificity of these processes and the characteristics of their individual elements.

This issue concerns especially the institution of health insurance, which has been losing its market character more and more over many decades. However, in order to be able to properly interpret these changes and their effects, it is first necessary to present the conditions necessary for the establishment and proper functioning of this institution. Insurance has certain limitations which prevent comprehensive financing of access to medical services for the whole society. However, it would be a mistake to perceive these limitations as a disadvantage of insurance – it is a more specific specificity of this institution. Therefore, it must be supported by other solutions, such as direct payments or charity.

It will also have a positive impact on the competition process and will allow us to avoid many problems present in universal (public systems), e.g. the lack of negative selection or moral hazard. Better understanding of the functioning of market solutions boils down to the appropriate presentation of the relationship between the various forms of financing access to medical services. The process of their free shaping allows for the emergence of a rational financing structure that does not exclude the most needy.

It is also important to present the so-called market failures, which are to be a fundamental obstacle preventing the application of market solutions in the indicated area.

DOI: 10.4324/9781003258957-2

1 Insurance as a market institution

Uncertainty as the main reason for the emergence of insurance

Uncertainty is inextricably linked to the future[1] and human action. Uncertainty, understood as the lack of complete certainty of a person as to the occurrence of future events in the real world, causes that they take action (engages appropriate resources) to satisfy their needs (remove discomfort), which is tantamount to the elimination or reduction of this uncertainty. The existence of uncertainty thus gives human action a speculative dimension.[2] The future may bring about events that improve or deteriorate an individual's situation. Humans show determination to learn about future conditions (recognizing opportunities and threats) as well as they possibly can, thanks to which they will be able to better meet their needs. Two main sources (spheres) of uncertainty can be identified: sufficiently unknown natural phenomena and human activities involving the selection of individual goals and means for their implementation (Mises, 1998, p. 105).

Thus, the mere existence of uncertainty does not limit human action. When trying to meet the challenges of the future, people use their knowledge, experience, and creativity in a unique way. As Huerta De Soto (2010, p. 15) points out: 'In a broad or general sense, entrepreneurship actually coincides with human action. In this respect, it could be said that any person who acts to modify the present and achieve his objectives in the future exercises entrepreneurship.'

Entrepreneurship can be considered as a key human skill for reducing or eliminating uncertainty. What can be considered a paradox, on the one hand, is that thanks to entrepreneurship, it is possible to eliminate a certain amount of uncertainty. On the other hand, entrepreneurship itself, especially at the stage of vision and creating new plans, widens this uncertainty. However, this kind of uncertainty is not pejorative, but gives hope for a better tomorrow.[3] For example, societies experiencing

DOI: 10.4324/9781003258957-3

constant improvement of their material conditions as a result of the industrial revolution were unable to indicate the exact direction of technological changes or specific inventions that would arise in the future, but they intuitively realized that these processes had already started and that positive results would occur in the near or distant future.

Uncertainty is so closely related to human existence that it is difficult to even imagine a reality in which the future is known exactly. There would be no room for human action in this kind of world. Entrepreneurship and economic calculation would not occur, as all possible activities and their effects would be known (discovered) in advance. In such a reality there would also be no space for the creation and development of an insurance institution. Certainty can be understood in two ways: that certain events may or may not happen. There is no third possibility, no option: the event may occur. In the first case, it is known, for example, who will set fire to the house and who will not, so people who have suffered the damage would receive compensation not so much from the insurance, but from predetermined (as to the time and amount of compensation) capital transfers from the rest of the society.[4] The insurer would not employ staff responsible for the identification, selection, or qualification of the risk. Professions such as underwriter or actuary would simply not exist. In a world of certainty, they would be an unnecessary expense. A similar situation would occur if certain events did not occur at all. If a given (negative) event does not occur, then there cannot be its cause that could cause adverse consequences for the individual. For example, in a world of complete certainty, car accidents or crashes would not happen, as they could be prevented in advance. The inability of a given event to occur in the future will not cause a feeling of uncertainty (discomfort) in an individual, which they will want to counteract by purchasing insurance.

Therefore, uncertainty should be considered the first, necessary factor, a kind of sphere in which, thanks to human entrepreneurship, the institution of insurance was established and evolved. At this point, however, it should be emphasized that the mere existence of uncertainty is not enough to create insurance, which is rightly associated with concepts such as probability and (especially) risk. Other essential conditions must therefore be met.

It is also worth mentioning that although the future and uncertainty are terms that are intuitively understood in the same way by most people, at the same time they are perceived differently by each person. In this sense, they are not homogeneous. Each person creates their own vision of the future (sets goals) and strives to implement it on the basis of their own actions. By implementing the previously assumed goals, the individual realizes their plans, but does not feel that their actions constitute a certain contribution to the overall future. Of course, people are aware of their similar needs. Most people dream of their own apartment or house, and in a world of scarcity of goods, entrepreneurs (producers) try to satisfy their needs in the best possible way. Recognition of the convergence of needs (and costs that consumers are able to incur) is therefore an important element of entrepreneurial activity and gives a chance to make a profit. The better entrepreneurs recognize the greater the convergence of needs and costs, the greater the chances for profits. This observation is also true and particularly relevant to the insurance market.

Probability and risk

Although the concepts of probability, risk, and uncertainty are inter-related, skilfully distinguishing them is an important step in understanding the origins of an insurance institution. The very concept of probability is quite general and assumes the possibility of a given event occurring in the future. However, some events, and more specifically the probability of their future occurrence, can be represented in terms, symbols, or mathematical models, which can facilitate decision-making in a world of uncertainty. The issue of the possibility of using numbers allows for two types of probability to be distinguished: the class probability and the case probability (Mises, 1998, p. 107).

Mises (1998, p. 107), who is the creator of the probability classification presented in this way, points out that:

> Class probability means: We know or assume to know, with regard to the problem concerned, everything about the behavior of a whole class of events or phenomena; but about the actual singular events or phenomena we know nothing but that they are elements of this class.

Let us assume that we have statistical data from the last several dozen years, which show that, for example, out of 10,000 houses, five catch fire each year. This information forms a class (group) of specific, homogeneous events. It is not known exactly which house will catch fire (we do not have any information on this), but it is assumed that in the following year their number will be the same, if there are no other factors increasing or reducing the likelihood of such an event. Similar conclusions can be drawn based, for example, on the average life expectancy of a given population. Although the average age of the members of a certain community is known and amounts to e.g. 78

years, on this basis it is not possible to estimate the life expectancy of its individual members. We have knowledge of the entire class of events, but we know nothing about its individual elements.

The situation is completely different in the case of case probability. Mises (1998, p. 110) states that:

> Case probability means: We know, with regard to a particular event, some of the factors which determine its outcome; but there are other determining factors about which we know nothing.
>
> Case probability has nothing in common with class probability but the incompleteness of our knowledge. In every other regard the two are entirely different.[5]

This type of probability has particular application in economics or more broadly in praxeology. Each act of human action is unique, in part because of the subjectivity of the value judgements of the acting individual. As Huerta De Soto (2010, p. 31) points out:

> Therefore, each time man acts and exercises entrepreneurship, he does so in a characteristic, personal, and unrepeatable manner all his own, a manner which arises from his attempt to gain certain objectives or arrive at a particular vision of the world, all of which act as incentives and which, in their particular form and circumstances, only he possesses. The above enables each human being to obtain certain knowledge or information which he discovers only depending on his ends and circumstances and which no other person can possess in an identical form.

This type of probability cannot be assigned to any class precisely due to the fact that these events are not homogeneous, but unique. In this approach, we cannot talk about the frequency (repeatability) of events as in the case of class probability. An example is a match between two football teams, such as Real Madrid and UD Levante. Real Madrid has a much bigger budget and better players. Every year it fights to get as many trophies as possible. In turn, Levante is a club with much lower aspirations, for which staying in the league is a satisfactory result. Simply put, it can be assumed that, taking into account the results of the past, in ten matches played between these teams, nine will end with a victory for Real, and in one the team from the Valencia suburbs will be able to draw or win. However, these data, in the perspective of the next match, do not allow for a completely certain conclusion that this will happen. When assessing these chances, the data from the past does not say anything about the next match; it only contains information about the course of events (match results) in the past, taking into account specific past conditions. It is not known whether the next game will be the one in which the team from Madrid will not be victorious. Of course, an objective observer will easily be able to tell that Real's chances of winning are definitely greater (due to the better soccer skills of its players) based on some of the information it has at its disposal. However, you can as well imagine that someone, after a thorough analysis, will 'risk' the statement that Levante will not lose the next match. What both have in common is that the final outcome predictions are based on incomplete data. If it were otherwise, the result would be known in advance.

A similar line of reasoning can also be applied to other cases where there is human action, such as decisions made by consumers (e.g. buying blue or black trousers), actions of entrepreneurs (uncertainty about making a profit), or presidential elections. All these cases are unique due to the fact that when making decisions, people are guided by reason – they do not react passively to external stimuli.[6]

Although the two types of probability are very different, it is possible to confuse the probability of individual events with that of classes. This error was described by Mises as the so-called gambler's fallacy. After diagnosing a specific disease in a patient, the doctor informs the patient that 5 out of 100 cases end in death during the treatment process. If the patient asks the doctor if these five people have already died, it means that they has succumbed to this delusion. Forecasting based on only part of the information covering one specific case is unreliable; therefore in such cases knowledge about the behaviour of the whole class is used. Therefore, if the prognosis of the patient's chances of survival is to be more reliable, it should be compared to other, similar cases (e.g. survival among men up to 30 years of age, etc.). Better examination of the patient will allow for obtaining more information and assigning them to a different class (determined on the basis of more criteria), but the prognosis for their health will still be based on the behaviour of the whole class (Mises, 1998, pp. 110–111).

Although the concept of risk does not appear in the quoted fragments on probability, the definition of class probability suits it well. In the literature, the term risk is usually associated with F. H. Knight, who is credited with distinguishing between risk and uncertainty (Knight, 1921, p. 233). We talk about risk when a given event can be classified into a sufficiently large class of the same events, and the frequency of occurrence of events belonging to this class can be determined with great certainty in a mathematical form, that is, presented by means of the probability calculus.[7] In the absence of such a possibility, according to Knight, we are dealing with uncertainty, i.e. events that cannot be represented by numbers. In other words, the difference between risk and uncertainty boils down to the possibility of presenting (expressing) the probability of these events occurring in the form of mathematical symbols. Interestingly, for Knight himself, this distinction only served to create his own probability classification. As Foss and Klein (2012, p. 84) point out:

> this particular distinction is only invoked in passing (1921: 21, 233). His fundamental argument, developed in chapter 7 of Knight (1921), involves a tripartite classification of the notion of probability into 'apriori probability,' 'statistical probability,' and 'estimated probability.' Situations that can be described epistemically in terms of the two first categories represent risk, while the third condition describes situations involving uncertainty.

Comparing the two classifications to each other, it can be concluded that the Misesian class probability corresponds to Knight's risk, and the case probability to uncertainty.[8] Obviously, this is not the only economic interpretation and classification of risk, probability, or uncertainty, but it introduces more clarity to the argument in question. In this aspect, it is also worth getting acquainted with, inter alia, the works of K. J. Arrow, who did not introduce a detailed distinction between risk and uncertainty and used both terms interchangeably (Klimczak, 2008, p. 65).[9]

For the creation and development of an insurance institution, the issue of the application of the probability theory is of key importance. The present state of the modern insurance market is inextricably linked with the evolution of insurance mathematics. It is thanks to the use of probability calculus and mathematical statistics that it is possible to calculate the amount of insurance premiums or the level of provisions. Without these mathematical 'tools', the possibilities of calculating insurance (actuarial) risk would be very limited, and the insurance activity itself would be reduced to standardizing the level of premiums and limiting rather than extending the scope of insurance. With insurance mathematics, some uncertainty becomes 'measurable', making it much easier for insurers and consumers to make decisions. Professor N. Ferguson (2008, p. 190), an expert in economic and political history, even argues that: 'In short, it was not merchants but mathematicians who were the true progenitors of modern insurance.'

Both the contracts between merchants agreeing to jointly cover losses resulting from the failure of trade expeditions and social institutions supporting their members financially as a result of unfavourable events in the future (e.g. death, accident, or disease) functioned more as a form of protection against an uncertain future as insurance.[10] However, it should be emphasized that before the development of mathematics brought about the creation of insurance,[11] these institutions were, considering the conditions of that time, particularly important for certain social groups, and even entire nations. It is difficult to imagine the development of trade between individual regions if merchants undertaking a long and dangerous journey would not have any security as a result of unfavourable events (e.g. sinking of ships carrying goods during a storm at sea). In the absence of a willingness to participate in losses, trade (and thus economic development) would develop much slower.

For insurers, the use of mathematical achievements is an indispensable element of economic calculation. This is one of the features that distinguishes insurers from 'ordinary' companies for which costing has a different dimension. If 'ordinary' entrepreneurs anticipate consumers' needs well, revenues will exceed costs and thus a profit will be generated. Costs incurred in the past (prices of production factors) do not have to be the same in the future; therefore the entrepreneurial function consists, among other things, in noticing factors that may influence these changes. However, the costs incurred in the past do not change; they are data and constant. The situation is slightly different in the case of insurers for whom some of the costs resulting from the insurance contract (e.g. future compensation payments due to fires) are not costs already incurred, e.g. purchase of raw materials in the case of 'traditional' activities, but planned (hypothetical) costs that will have to be incurred in the future. In this case, the insurer is not entirely sure about their amount. This part of the economic calculation relates to class probability, therefore an insurer needs skilled workers (especially actuaries and underwriters)[12] to specialize in the economic calculation process based on this probability, in other words, in the process of identifying, selecting, and classifying actuarial risks. Of course, decisions regarding for example the strategy and directions of development of a given insurance company, marketing campaigns, or the creation of new insurance products are an example of the probability of individual events and they concern all entrepreneurs. Rothbard (2009, p. 555) put it this way: 'Estimates of future costs, demands, etc., on the part of entrepreneurs are all unique cases of uncertainty, where methods of specific understanding and individual judgment of the situation must apply, rather than objectively measurable or insurable "risk".'

However, in addition, insurance companies, which is their special feature, also make extensive use of a particular type of economic calculation based on class probability. Insurers compete for customers with other enterprises not only in terms of the price and quality of insurance products, but also through a different type and quality of economic calculation. Examples include an insurer that offers private health insurance and a medical network that sells medical subscriptions. Although these products may have a similar range of medical services and prices, the process of their production and calculation was completely different. The insurer is looking for a competitive advantage also in the area of the form of economic calculation; other enterprises also use it, but it is not so much based on class probability.[13]

One important feature of risk is that it is a component of complex economic phenomena and so does this over time. In this respect, the risk can be described as successive phases, which makes it more dynamic than static. Therefore, the concept of risk should not be reduced only to the theory of probability. The following stages can be mentioned that constitute risk understood as a process taking place in time: threat, danger, realization of danger, loss, mental reaction, emotional reaction, behavioural reaction. In the case of the first four stages, one can speak of objective risk, i.e. the risk where the calculus of probability applies. The other three, on the other hand, qualify for the so-called subjective risk, subject to human value judgements (Kowalewski, 2001, p. 35). In the latter case, however, the use of the term 'risk' may be misleading because, as discussed earlier, the subjective human evaluations are unique and cannot be represented in terms of classes.[14]

The threat as a potential source of risk may come from the action of natural forces or human activity. For example, driving a car, despite the undoubted benefits this brings to its owners, may lead to a road accident. The sources of danger and risk may be, for example, unfavourable weather conditions or careless driving by the driver. As a result of such an event, property and often personal damage may occur. The resulting damage would undoubtedly result in financial losses and the loss of a part of the victim's property. The existence of a person's awareness of a possible unfavourable development of events (mental reaction) can lead to anxiety (emotional reaction) while driving a car. As a result, such a person may be more inclined to purchase life insurance or motor insurance (behavioural reaction). From the economic perspective, the last three stages are not so important because the act of acting itself is more important, i.e. making an informed decision as to whether or not to purchase insurance. Identifying these specific incentives can be useful to some extent in economics if risk is to be shown as a process over time. The second stage is more important for the marketing activities of insurance companies trying to attract the attention of potential customers, which undoubtedly contributes to the development of the insurance market.

At this point, another important feature of the insurance institution should be mentioned. The primary purpose of insurance is to compensate the insured for losses resulting from certain unfavourable future events (random events). Therefore, the amount of the sum insured (and thus the insurance premium) is adjusted to the material and financial situation of the insured. Any deviation from the optimal sum insured may be considered underinsurance or overinsurance. In his work on insurance and risk, Mowbray indicates a significant risk division: pure risk and speculative risk (Mowbray & Blanchard, 1961, pp. 6–7).

In the case of pure risk, characteristic of the insurance market, there is no loss (non-realization of risk) or loss (realization of risk resulting in loss). The insured allocates appropriate funds in the form of insurance premiums; however, according to the exchange theory, it is a favourable situation for them – he gains insurance protection in an uncertain future for them. Importantly, the insured cannot make a profit in the event of a loss. It is completely different in the case of speculative risk. Here, in addition to loss or no loss, it is possible to make a profit. The action taken is because there is hope for profit. Examples of such activities include participation in gambling (e.g. roulette) or the purchase of certain assets (e.g. real estate, shares, etc.) with the hope of selling them at a higher price in the near or distant future (Outerville, 1998, p. 3). The difference between these two types of risk is that none of the insured want to take the pure risk, while the realization of speculative risk is not pejorative for the player. It can be concluded that the chance of making a profit means that a person can, through their conscious actions, strive to increase the chances of its implementation. Thus, a person tries to create a speculative risk and at the same time reduce the probability of pure risk (e.g. healthier eating as a method to reduce the risk of a heart attack). Therefore, common underwriting risks are assigned pure risk traits where class probability applies. In turn, speculative risk can be equated with both the case probability and the class probability.

At this point, it is worth mentioning that another important feature that distinguishes an insurance institution is its group character. The use of insurance mathematics is used by insurers to create, based on separate criteria, specific risk classes (groups) that differ from each other, e.g. in the amount of premium or the scope of insurance. Although individual classes differ in the level of risk, i.e. they are not homogeneous, the common feature of all of them is the group character created by individual units belonging to specific classes.[15]

Therefore, insurance companies strive to acquire new insured as soon as possible and create real (numerous, mass) risk groups. If the insurer enters into an insurance contract with only one person, it will not be considered insurance, but gambling.[16] While in the described situation the probability calculation applies, the lack of other insured persons means that in the event of an insured event, the insurer has to cover the resulting losses from equity (and thus maintain a higher level of provisions). That is why it is so important to create a large group as soon as possible when introducing new insurance products to the market. The larger the group (the more insured), the greater the predictability of events (the law of large numbers), i.e. the greater the stability of the insurance company. Of course, there are situations when the insurer has to wait until a certain (longer) period has passed and a sufficiently large group of insured persons has been formed. Such cases include, for example, 'insurance' of the vocal cords of individual singers, or even 'insurance' of certain parts of the body of sports stars. However, the actions of insurers consisting in creating sufficiently numerous risk groups as soon as possible should be considered an economically justified rule.

On the basis of the content presented above, it can be concluded that insurance is a market institution that uses advanced economic calculation (based in particular on the probability calculation) in order to compensate (according to predetermined rules) losses resulting from certain adverse events to one insured with funds from the invested premiums of all insured persons included in a given risk group (class), in particular those who were not covered by the given events.

Health as a subject of insurance

One of the types of adverse event resulting in losses for the insured person is loss of health (e.g. as a result of an accident or illness). The related discomfort causes a person to want to recover as soon as possible, and insurance should be considered one of the measures to achieve this goal. However, in order for an appropriate insurance product of this type to be created, first of all, it is necessary to define what health is and how its loss may result in the consumption of insurance.

One of the most frequently quoted definitions of health is the one introduced by the World Health Organization (WHO, no date) in 1948. According to this: 'Health is a state of complete physical, mental and social well-being and not merely the absence of disease or infirmity.' This definition draws attention to the fact that health can be understood as active human activities aimed at maintaining its current state or even improving (even better quality), and not only considering health as a certain lost value and the desire to restore it from the moment of the onset of the disease. However, this approach has its limitations and problems. The use of the word 'complete' in the cited definition is particularly critical. 'Full' means that any deviations are treated as a non-health condition, which may result in excessive focus on the development and use of technology or drugs in situations that often do not require it. As a result, specific medical procedures apply to entire groups rather than individual members. Therefore, these are not economic solutions. Another problem is that as a result of, inter alia, the development of medicine, it has become possible to live with chronic diseases or, to put it another way, to develop a chronic disease; although it is a personal drama for many people, it does not have the same serious consequences as it used to be. Thanks to the progress of medicine, it is possible for many people to pursue their professional career despite the presence of chronic diseases. Therefore, these people contribute to creating added value in the economy and treating them as sick or unfit for work is not appropriate due to their adaptability (Huber et al., 2011, p. D4163).

The border between health and disease does not have to be sharp and unambiguous, but reflections on the definition of health, possible thanks to the development of medical knowledge, should increasingly take into account the factors contributing to the health–disease dichotomy and the possible consequences of this state of affairs.

For insurance companies, the problem of recognizing health comes down to, inter alia, defining the conditions justifying the use of medical services by the insured or receiving a cash benefit. As the insurance is intended to compensate for the loss (loss of health), the incident causing it cannot, by definition, occur before the insurance period. That is why the assessment of the health condition of people applying for insurance is so important. It is also important how the loss is to be compensated. On this basis, sickness and accident insurance can be distinguished as a special type of health insurance, which involves the payment of predefined cash benefits to the insured in connection with the occurrence of specific events. However, with so-called medical insurance,[17] the insured receives access to medical services, financed by the insurance company, instead of cash. Medical services are usually provided by specific medical facilities that cooperate with the insurance company (Osak, 2008, p. 163). Both types of insurance can be offered in parallel. Sickness and accident insurance compensate the insured for financial losses resulting, for example, from loss of earnings during treatment, while medical insurance covers the costs of medical services. Medical insurance is beneficial in this respect, as it is the insurance company that is responsible for organizing the structure responsible for treating the insured, which undoubtedly shortens the initial process and improves the quality of the insurance product.

Economic calculation based on probability plays an extremely important role in the process of creating health insurance (especially medical insurance). It is applied in two stages. The first stage concerns the calculation of the very probability of a given event (e.g. disease) occurring in the future. In turn, in the second stage, it is extremely important to estimate the costs of using specific medical procedures (and their effectiveness) in the treatment process. Medical insurance differs in this respect, for example, from life insurance in that the insurance risk, and more specifically the process of its calculation, is more complex and the mere use of insurance mathematics to determine only the quantitative probability of a given event is not sufficient. Even if the risk of developing a given disease in a particular group (class) of people is determined with high probability, the sphere of calculation, including the impact of individual treatment methods (and their costs) on the improvement of the insured's health, is equally important.

It is possible that the risk of a given disease can be determined, but at the same time the current state of medical knowledge does not allow for a rational calculation of treatment costs. It can therefore be concluded that for a given disease it is not possible to make a rational economic calculation in the second stage. Therefore, it cannot be determined whether the initially estimated level of the contribution is appropriate, too high, or too low. As a result, a given risk is considered, in the present circumstances, as insurable. Guzel (2013b, p. 125)[18] claims that:

> an example of such a disease is discopathy, which can take many years to develop and cause complaints of varying severity. The scope of potential changes found in the spine in people with discopathy and their impact on the risk of incapacity for work are so extensive that it is practically impossible to rationally estimate the level of the necessary increase in the insurance premium (e.g. due to the lack of appropriate clinical trials). Therefore, it seems that the best solution is to apply an appropriate exclusion.

In the case of life insurance, it is much easier to estimate the potential costs resulting from the death of the insured person and thus the sum insured on the basis of the insured's income or the amount of financial liabilities (e.g. a loan). The economic calculation taking into account the calculation of probability in life insurance concerns mainly the first stage.

In the case of health insurance, both stages of the calculation are preceded by a thorough scientific analysis, especially the research carried out on the appropriate group of people.[19] It can be concluded that the process of obtaining data, analysing them and using the knowledge thus acquired in order to determine risk is the initial stage of economic calculation. The successively growing medical knowledge allows insurers to better and better calculate risk and thus to compete by creating more 'advanced' risk groups (classes). The processes based on the appropriate use of medical knowledge in the development of health insurance are called Evidence Based Underwriting (EBU) and are derived from medicine based on reliable (i.e. scientifically supported) data (Evidence Based Medicine – EBM) (Lipka, 2013a, pp. 94–98). Properly verified medical knowledge allows, among other things, the development of more effective procedures that can be used in the treatment of specific diseases and, ultimately, to include them in the scope of medical insurance. Thus, it can be concluded that developing medicine affects the quality of economic calculation.[20] Therefore, insurers are interested in the latest results of research concerning, for example, the effectiveness of the use of new medical procedures in the treatment of selected diseases, as well as scientific studies focusing on forecasting specific trends, e.g. concerning the eating habits of the population. It should be emphasized that the constantly growing number of scientific publications is a great challenge for insurers and requires the involvement of more and more human resources and their proper management.

The health insurance market as an effect of entrepreneurial processes

The core of insurers' business is risk calculation. Its purpose is to adjust the amount of the net insurance premium[21] to the risk group (class) represented by the insured person. Each insurance company creates its own risk groups based on appropriate criteria, thanks to which it is possible to define rules for the appropriate calculation and assessment of insurance risk, including health risk. Often the activity of insurance companies is equated with collecting premiums from the insured and activities consisting in fulfilling the insurance contract to a limited extent, which is to be a source of their profit. This is a misconception. The basic assumption of the insurer is the payment of compensation or benefits due to the occurrence of a given event. Risk is inherent in the real world and its implementation results in a loss. One of the ways to eliminate or reduce the negative effects of risk implementation is insurance. Insurance companies, using an advanced economic calculation taking into account probability, are able to determine with increasing accuracy what factors cause a higher (or lower) probability of a given event. Thanks to this, they can distinguish further groups (classes) of risk from one general group. These groups differ in terms of risk and, as a result, the amount of insurance premiums. The higher the likelihood of a given event (e.g. a serious illness) occurring, the higher the likelihood of consuming the necessary medical services and, consequently, the insurance itself. Therefore, young and (in the opinion of the insurer) healthy people pay relatively lower premiums than the elderly and those who are already sick. An insurer that, in the conditions of an unfettered market economy, restricts access to certain benefits denies the sense of having insurance and is replaced by competitors that are more enterprising, i.e. better at calculating risk.

Although there may be a lot of individual risk groups,[22] each insurance company uses a basic division into the so-called standard risk and substandard risk. The first type means a risk that is accepted by the insurer without premium increases, while the substandard risk means admission to insurance, but after taking into account the premium increases (Lipka, 2013b, p. 117). Subsequently, the insurer may create further subgroups for standard risk (e.g. S1, S2, S3, etc.) and for substandard risk (e.g. Sb1, Sb2, Sb3, etc.). The ability to properly calculate risk and create appropriate risk groups (classes) based on it is the main tool for creating a competitive advantage on the market. Therefore, the insurer does not strive to limit substandard risk only to its appropriate calculation. The rule according to which the premium paid is proportional to the risk represented by the insured person is called the 'principle of fairness' (Guzel, 2013a, p. 99) and constitutes the basis for the stability of the functioning of insurance companies.[23]

Appropriate risk assessment[24] is of particular importance in the case of health insurance. Unlike, for example, life insurance, health insurance may be consumed many times. Moreover, the frequency of using medical services may result not only from the deterioration of the insured's health, but also from certain habits. This is a big challenge for insurance companies due to the fact that it is very difficult to identify people who use health insurance without valid reasons, and it is even more difficult to change this state (Kostrzewski, 2013, pp. 140–141). Moreover, the insurer cannot change the rules of using the insurance during its term, which makes the risk assessment process[25] so important.

An error in the form of wrong premium estimation or inadequate risk classification may result in losses for the insurance company and, as a result, deterioration of access to medical services. Obtaining information about the health of the insured person is of particular importance for the insurer, as it is mainly on this basis that decisions are made whether and on what terms a given person may be covered by insurance. If the risk assessment did not take into account the factors that could affect the terms of the insurance, the so-called anti-selection occurred.[26] This phenomenon has two causes. The first is the low quality of the risk assessment by the insurer itself, which leads to an incorrect determination of the amount of premiums or the scope of insurance. Usually, the insurer is quick to understand the situation and improves the quality of the risk assessment. On the other hand, the second reason is more difficult to eliminate, because its source is deliberate concealment of information by the person applying for insurance protection. It can therefore be concluded that the source of anti-selection is the asymmetry of information between the insurer and the insured. The insurer, wishing to counteract such practices, undertakes a number of actions aimed at eliminating or at least limiting anti-selection. These include, in particular, the establishment of an appropriate level of co-payment,[27] i.e. the costs incurred by the insured when using the insurance. Other possible actions include, for example, the introduction of limits on the use of medical services or the application of exclusions of certain risks from insurance protection. Such activities, although they may be misunderstood by part of the public, are essential to the creation of solid insurance products. An emotional approach to insurers' practices (e.g. foreclosure) may obscure the fact that risks would otherwise be uneconomically grouped. For example, persons with a sub-standard risk would be admitted to insurance on a standardized basis and, as a result, would pay a premium that is inadequate to the risk contributed. This would result in over-consumption of medical services and increase costs. Subsequently, the insurer would have to increase premiums to cover the rising costs, but some insured persons could then opt out of insurance.

Therefore, in order to avoid such situations, the insurer must be able to limit or completely eliminate intentional actions of some insured persons, otherwise known as moral hazard. Moral hazard can be defined as the insured's deliberate action aimed at bringing them tangible benefits (e.g. concealing information about their health in order to be accepted for insurance or pay a lower premium), but without incurring the costs of such actions. Such attitudes are not any form of restoring greater social justice and, it is worth emphasizing, they do not hit only insurers, but most of all other insured people (which is too rarely mentioned). It is on them, as a last resort, that the additional costs of such activities are passed on – honest customers of insurance companies subsidize those who are tempted to abuse.[28] If someone claims that paying higher premiums by sick people is unethical, then one should consider whether a young and relatively healthy person should incur higher costs with a low probability of using insurance. It can be concluded from this that insurance companies also care about the interests of their clients who have trusted them. Anti-selection or moral hazard, which is not dealt with, may cause financial problems for insurers and, ultimately, loss of the trust of the insured. It is not a win-win situation.

In the health insurance market, the laws of the economy work the same as in other markets. Purchasing insurance is an act of exchange that benefits both parties. The insured person receives a guarantee that in the event of a given event (e.g. an accident), they will be able to count on the insurance to obtain access to specific medical services. Their belief is not unfounded. The insurer, thanks to the appropriate risk assessment and the ability to reduce the moral hazard, is able to create a stable insurance programme, thanks to which it can achieve profit from the invested premiums. The greater freedom of action the insurer has, the greater the stability of insurance programmes, and thus the more secure access to medical services for the insured. The insured person who pays the insurance premium covers not only the administrative costs borne by the insurer, the costs constituting the commission for financial intermediaries, or the costs constituting the remuneration of entities providing medical services, but they also finance access to these services for those insured who have been affected by certain events (e.g. accident or illness). For example, if a person with a good health condition has been correctly classified to a given risk group, e.g. to the standard risk group S1, and other insured persons in this group will also represent the same risk, then such insurance will be able to adequately meet their needs. On the other hand, if the S1 risk group includes a certain number of people representing the Sb1 substandard risk (e.g. due to concealing information about their health condition), the insurer will have to allocate more funds to finance medical services and increase the premium. For some of the insured with standard risk S1, it may turn out to be too high and they will not be interested in further insurance coverage. Hence, specific actions of the insurer are fully understandable, because by creating appropriate risk groups, differentiating premiums, or applying exclusions, they care for the interests of their clients. On this basis, it can be concluded that, in economic terms, it is not so much the insurer excludes its clients as its clients exclude themselves. If an insurer does not meet their expectations, its competitors will. Nobody who is relatively healthy wants to overpay for an extensive health insurance package that they do not use, but that only pays extra money to people who frequently use medical services.

This is in line with the theory of price imputation, which says that productive goods have value because they can produce the consumer (end) goods and services that consumers desire. Entrepreneurs (including insurance companies) bear certain costs, because they assume that the price they offer for their products will be accepted by customers (insured) and will allow them to cover the costs and achieve the assumed profit. The prices of consumer goods and services are therefore a derivative of the preferences of consumers who are ready to buy them (Machaj, 2013, p. 109). Therefore, the consumer pays attention to the benefits of consuming the final product. They do not think about the costs of the factors of production that were involved in the production of a given good or service. It is similar in the case of insurance, where the insured expects an appropriate price and quality of insurance and does not reflect on the risk group they are in. They compare the given insurance to the competition's offer and selects the best option for themself, or they do not purchase the insurance at all, if they are not satisfied with any offer.

Importantly, while the use of exclusions in health insurance excludes this form of access to medical services (or may limit the choice between individual offers of insurers), it does not prohibit such access at all. Health insurance should therefore not be seen as a form of access to such services, but rather as a form of financing that access. Insurance in itself does not increase the supply of doctors, drugs, or new medical devices. Thanks to insurance, it is possible to transfer funds from people who were not affected by a given event to those to whom it happened to cover the costs of treatment. If, for some reason, the number of doctors, medical facilities, or medical equipment remains constant, but the number of insured consumers who consume medical services is growing, costs will increase or even visit limits will be introduced. The benefits of health insurance should not obscure the fact that it is only one form of financing access to specific medical services. Therefore, it should be remembered that in the conditions of the market economy, people who, for various reasons, cannot be covered by insurance are not deprived of it at all, only the form of (financing) access to these services changes. The more developed individual market institutions are, the easier these processes occur.

Exclusions in the health insurance market are nothing special, as they are in the rest of the economy. Owing to exclusions, it is possible to establish property rights enabling a rational calculation of the factors of production. The price system also reflects the economic nature of goods and services. High prices reflect the relationship between supply and demand – they inform about the unavailability of certain goods and, in a way, force their economical use. Exclusions and limitations are one of the foundations of civilization and the economy (Rockwell, 2012). A car manufacturer negotiating a new contract with its suppliers has the right to withdraw from the contract if it deems that it does not meet its expectations. If this is not done, the final product may turn out to be worse than the competition and the producer will suffer losses. Likewise, the consumer has the right not to buy a given product if they deem it not worth the price. What seems to be a paradox, it is thanks to exclusions that it becomes possible to maintain a certain unity and solidarity between members of particular groups. It is of particular importance for the health insurance market, because due to the correct risk assessment and a number of other activities of insurance companies, the insured will be convinced that their interests are looked after. Thanks to this, they will continue to pay contributions. Insurance companies will gain their recognition and reputation of stable institutions that can be relied on in difficult situations. Departure from this principle will not result in greater social justice, but only in favouring certain social groups at the expense of others and the disappearance of the insurance institution. The question of the trust of members who make up particular social groups, although he did not directly mean insurance, was well expressed by Sinek (2009, pp. 114, 122):

> only when individuals can trust the culture or organization will they take personal risks in order to advance that culture or organization as a whole. [...] When we believe someone has our best interest in mind because it is in their benefit to do so, the whole group benefits.

This is especially important as the loss of even a small number of customers can result in losses for insurers. Usually, people who are already ill, who try to access certain medical services at a low cost, are more interested in joining health insurance. Insurance is a more economical option for them than, for example, direct payments. They may also be more determined to continue insurance, even in the case of constantly increasing premiums. On the other hand, relatively healthy people do not show that much interest in purchasing insurance, as they relatively rarely use medical services. The difficult role of the insurer is to rationally evaluate the health risk for these particular groups. The higher frequency of using health insurance by the insured means that even a small loss of some insured (e.g. persons representing standard risk) may result in losses for the insurer. For example, it is indicated that in the United States of America, which has several types of private health insurance and public programmes, 10% of the population consumes about 72% of healthcare expenditure, and 2% of the population consumes 41% of healthcare expenditure (Light, 2000, pp. 969–974). The situation is similar in Poland, where, according to the data of the National Health Fund for 2009, only 5% of the insured in the public system generated 60% of all costs. In turn, treatment of 75% of the insured accounted for about 10% of expenses (Dzielak et al., 2010, p. 4). These data show that a relatively small proportion of the insured are able to generate most of the expenses.[29] Therefore, in commercial insurance, where contracts are voluntarily concluded, risk assessment is of such special importance. Therefore, the insurer's risk is not that a given event will take place, but whether the frequency of such events (e.g. diseases or the intensity of using medical services by the insured) falls within the framework assumed by the insurer. The insurer assumes that a given event will take place and monitors the level of deviations that occur at the same time. In other words, for the insurer, the risk will be, for example, that during the insurance period a greater number of people fall ill than assumed, which will affect the level of treatment costs.

However, in the health insurance market, a situation is possible where the insurer's portfolio is dominated by sub-standard risks, if the insured classified to particular sub-standard risk groups accept an increased premium for the insurance. Insurance coverage may even apply to events taking place in the past, if special conditions allow it, e.g. in group insurance concluded at the workplace, all employees usually form one risk group with one, average premium. It also often happens that the employer pays part or even all of the premium. However, this does not change the nature of the insurance, as the insurer continues to use advanced risk assessment and constantly monitors the use of medical services by the insured. Even if a certain group of employees who were ill before uses insurance, it is possible thanks to contributions paid by other employees and the employer. If the insurer has not made a mistake and there is acceptance among employees for incurring appropriate costs, such an insurance programme, although it has its limitations,[30] is possible.

Insurers also offer health insurance against very rare risks that affect a relatively small percentage of a given population. However, if such a risk occurs, the person concerned will not be able to cover the costs incurred by themself. Then having insurance makes sense, and the insurer is relatively easy to assess such a risk, as it does not occur as often as, for example, the flu. Such events include the risk of developing leukaemia. It is a very rare disease, but its occurrence is very costly (Berdine, 2011).

Insurance companies also play a very important role in the accumulation and allocation of capital in the economy. The creation and evolution of an insurance institution can also be associated with a low time preference. In the absence of insurance, a person may take action of gradual accumulation of certain amounts of money towards the uncertain future. The larger the amounts and if the accumulated capital continues to grow, the lower the time preference will be for a given person. On the other hand, insurance allows for a significant shortening of this process; they are more attractive, among others, because they allow for faster accumulation of the necessary funds in a certain group of people. Insured persons do not have to be afraid that the occurrence of an undesirable event will occur at a time when they have not yet managed to save adequate funds, as parallel payments of all insured persons significantly accelerate this process. Thus, insurance causes a significant intensification of the positive effects associated with low time preference. Insurance companies that conduct a reliable risk assessment, as a result, have significant capital, which they allocate (invest) appropriately depending on the type of risk. The lower the frequency of the events, the longer the investment will be. On the other hand, if there is a significant degree of consumption of insurance in a given insurance programme, then the time horizon of such investments is shortened. To some extent, it reflects the attitudes of the insured and the quality of the assessment and risk management of insurance companies. The positive contribution of insurance institution to the development of the capital structure of the economy was also noticed by Mises (2006, p. 86), who stated that:

> A great part of the capital at work in American enterprises is owned by the workers themselves and by other people with modest means. Billions and billions of saving deposits, of bonds, and of insurance policies are operating in these enterprises. On the American money market today, it is no longer the banks, it is the insurance companies that are the greatest money lenders. And the money of the insurance company is—not legally, but economically—the property of the insured. And practically everybody in the United States is insured in one way or another.

It is worth emphasizing that in the economic sense, insurance companies do not perform the so-called transfer of risk, both when accepting a given person for insurance and when investing the funds raised (net premiums). It is not true to say that the essence of insurance companies' activity is the transfer of risk. Conclusion of the insurance contract will not result in the insured person no longer having to worry about unfavourable events, as these have been transferred to the insurance company from the moment the policy was in force. The insurance does not eliminate or postpone the causes causing the given events. It only allows the reduction or elimination of negative effects resulting from the realization of a given risk. As already mentioned, the role of insurance is to cover the insured's losses. It is the insurer, not the insured person, who bears the costs related to the occurrence of a given event, but it is by no means a transfer of risk. Risk occurs over time; it is not a good that can be transferred from point A to point B. The expression risk transfer has a certain metaphorical meaning here and as such is used in the insurance industry – which is probably intended to be a simplified term for covering losses incurred by the insured due to the materialization of a given risk. However, it has no application for economics.[31] The functioning of insurers on the health insurance market requires the coordination of many complex processes. Individual insurance companies compete with each other for clients on many levels, ranging from the quality of economic calculation using probability, and ending with marketing or sales channels. However, it should be taken into account that despite the development of the health insurance market, there are still some factors that effectively prevent a given insurance product from entering the market. At times, these factors may be misinterpreted and misinterpreted. Such a case includes the arguments provided by Hoppe (2009) on the conditions necessary for the creation of health insurance:

> Private enterprise can offer insurance against events over whose outcome the insured possesses no control. One cannot insure oneself against suicide or bankruptcy, for example, because it is in one's own hands to bring these events about. Because a person's health, or lack of it, lies increasingly within his own control, many, if not most health risks, are actually uninsurable. 'Insurance' against risks whose likelihood an individual can systematically influence falls within that person's own responsibility.

While the arguments cited in the text by Hoppe regarding the elimination of state regulations in such areas of healthcare as medical universities educating future doctors or in the production of drugs and medical equipment should be considered correct, in the case of deregulation of the health insurance industry, the presented arguments are not appropriate. First of all, it should be noted, referring to Lipka (2013a, p. 87), that 'Modern methods of insurance risk assessment enable protection of 97–99% of people applying for insurance, including many people burdened with various health risk factors'.

Hoppe's arguments referring to having or not having control of the insured over their health as a prerequisite for health insurance are very imprecise. How can the insurer (and the insured themself) check when this control exists and when not? However, as it has already been presented, insurance companies create individual risk groups not on the basis of a clearly defined border defining some kind of awareness of the insured as to the control of their health, but on the basis of an appropriate risk calculation. Clients who deliberately try to deteriorate their health in order to receive an appropriate benefit are certainly characterized by pathological behaviours. However, their exclusion from insurance coverage is determined by economic calculation, namely the lack of acceptance of other insured persons who do not want to incur higher premiums. The abstract dichotomy has control – no control has no application here. On the other hand, how can you then explain people who were ill previously, but already accepted for insurance? Exactly the same principle as before. Of course, in this case it is no longer possible to talk about insurance risk, but about certainty, because the insurer is sure that such persons will immediately benefit from medical services. However, further, such an entity will calculate the risk due to having in its portfolio people with standard or sub-standard risk, who may voluntarily subsidize those who are already ill. Events covered by insurance are otherwise known as random events and, as Kowalewski (2001, p. 56) points out:

> What is a normal result of human action, in particular action taken to cause such an event, cannot be considered a random event. The random event must occur independently or against the will of the person affected by the event.

Perhaps this is what Hoppe meant, but his argument seems to be oversimplifying. For example, an insurer by offering insurance covering the costs of treatment abroad offers the client an additional extension of the insurance cover by random events resulting from the consumption of small amounts of alcohol. Therefore, the insured party consuming alcohol is aware that the probability of an accident is greater, and although it does not strive to cause it directly, the line between controlling and not controlling the risk begins to blur. In turn, the insurer can offer such an extension based on an appropriate risk calculation and a clear definition of the terms of its liability.

Therefore, in order for health insurance to arise, a given event must first be insurable, i.e. it must be possible to apply the calculus of probability. Otherwise, the event will be uninsurable, i.e. it will not be possible to rationally estimate the insurance premium. Subsequently, it is possible to indicate the insured risk and the uninsured risk. The insured risk occurs when it is possible to create a sufficiently large risk group. In the absence of a sufficient number of applicants, although a premium calculation is possible, the risk in question is not insured.

It seems that the use of an inadequate description of the rules governing the functioning of the health insurance market may lead to unnecessary misunderstandings with representatives of the insurance industry and ultimately hinder the introduction of necessary changes. The above remarks are particularly important as the individual stages of the health-care reform in the United States postulated by Hoppe are often eagerly quoted by Austrian School economists in various types of discussions and polemics. For example, Rothbard (2006, p. 133) points out that: 'Ludwig von Mises Institute, instead of offering its own 500-page health plan, sticks to its principled "four-step" plan laid out by Hans-Hermann Hoppe (Free Market, April 1993) of dismantling existing government intervention into health.' Therefore, for greater transparency of such activities, it is necessary to thoroughly analyse the arguments presented by Hoppe, which ultimately refer to the proposed changes on the health insurance market (in the United States of America).

Private and universal (public) health insurance

Insurance is a market institution, that is, one that was established and evolved on the basis of cooperation. Private health insurance cannot be confused with the so-called universal (public) health insurance, which is part of the social policy of states. In fact, there are a number of differences between private insurance and so-called public insurance.

First, insurance companies use advanced economic calculation using probability calculus to estimate risk and determine appropriate premiums for individual risk groups. Diversifying premiums, the scope of insurance, introducing exclusions and limitations is aimed at incurring costs in an adequate proportion to the obtained and invested premiums. The cooperation between the actuarial[32] and underwriting[33] departments allows for such risk management that enables profit. In the case of so-called public insurance, there is no risk calculation, selection, or classification. A uniform, compulsory premium is paid for all insured persons.[34] Public institutions responsible for financing access to healthcare do not have to fear the loss of insured persons. This situation makes the problem of moral hazard much more visible in public health programmes, especially when public authorities, in order to maintain them, often invoke the so-called right to healthcare of citizens.

Secondly, in the case of health insurance, it is usually unknown who specifically will need access to medical services. The insurance company is able to determine that, for example, out of 100,000 insured persons, 1% will develop a specific disease, but it is not known exactly who these people will be. In turn, in public insurance, in addition to such people, there is already a well-known, sick group of people. There is therefore no risk distribution, only certainty.

Thirdly, insurance companies, apart from financing access to a range of medical services for insured persons, invest some of the premiums obtained from them. As a result, the supply of savings increases on the market, which makes it easier for enterprises to raise the capital necessary to create more efficient production. Meanwhile, the so-called public insurance premiums are immediately consumed by the insured. Thus, the insurance market contributes to an increase in the supply of savings and their appropriate allocation in the economy,[35] while public insurance is nothing more than a redistribution of income. Compulsory transfer of funds between different groups of insured persons is not a source of investment.

Fourth, thanks to the limitations contained in the insurance contract, it is possible to rationally consume medical services. The insured know the limitations of such insurance, so they undertake other activities aimed at least maintaining their current state of health (e.g. they eat better). However, rational consumption of such services should not be equated with their rationing, which is characteristic of public programmes. In addition to insurance, there are many other forms of financing access to medical services and institutions offering them (e.g. medical networks, charities, or direct payments) in the unregulated market. Therefore, the lack of insurance does not mean that it is not possible to use medical services at all. Public insurance does not give the person in need of medical services a choice, and their situation worsens if they cannot avail themselves of these services through a public programme. For such people, only private insurance or other private institutions offering medical services are a real alternative.

Fifthly, in market conditions there are mechanisms contributing to the reduction of costs and improvement of the quality of medical services, which in the case of public insurance does not have to be so certain and often leads to an increase in costs or a decrease in the quality of services.

The above differences show that the so-called universal (public) insurance operates on extremely different principles than private insurance and there are, in principle, no common features between them, apart from the name. The first type of insurance is inextricably linked with interventionism. The second type is the result of market processes. Due to the above differences, it is not possible to combine these two types of insurance. Successive interventions in the health insurance market bring them closer to fulfilling a redistributive function in terms of financing access to medical services. The so-called universal (public) health insurance, which is an element of state policy, is not insurance in the true sense of the word. They have never been and never will be. Insurance, like money, is a market institution.

Notes

1 This is also true for sciences dealing with the past, such as history. While it is concerned with past events, the same study is an act of action. The uncertainty in this respect is therefore closely related to the desire to find answers (in the future) to the questions troubling historians. For example, what influenced the fall of the Roman Empire more? Barbarian invasions or internal (economic) problems? It is also a matter of historians looking for relevant information on this subject, which broadens their knowledge and reduces the aforementioned uncertainty.

2 Therefore, speculation should be broadly defined – as deliberate actions leading a person to achieve their goal under conditions of uncertainty. Therefore, this term does not have the colloquial and negative meaning so often ascribed to it.

3 Even if the trader made a mistake, the resulting loss would reveal it very quickly. Errors cannot be avoided, but the profit and loss mechanism, allows for their quick identification, which, at the same time, gives the competition a chance to take the place of those producers who were less able to predict the needs of consumers.

4 It would not even be compensation paid in money, but in abstract units of account. For more on this, see: Mises (1998, p. 250).

5 It is worth mentioning that Mises relied on the work of his brother Richard, an eminent mathematician. R. von Mises made an important contribution to the theory of probability. In his study 'Probability, Statistics, and Truth', he created an objective or 'frequency' theory of probability, so one that can be expressed numerically, which corresponds to L. von Mises' class probability. For more on this, see R. Mises (1981); Rothbard (1975).

6 It can be concluded that Shakespeare's 'To be or not to be? That is the question' perfectly captures the nature of Mises's case probability. Although, in this 'case', there are only two possible end results, the number of (unique) ways to achieve any of them cannot be estimated and grouped into appropriate classes.

 7 This is a slightly modified version of the definition of risk used by M. N. Rothbard: '"Risk" occurs when an event is a member of a class of a large number of homogeneous events and there is fairly certain knowledge of the frequency of occurrence of this class of events' (Rothbard, 2009, p. 552).

 8 For more on this, see: Hoppe (2007, pp. 1–20).

 9 For more on this, see: Arrow (1971).

10 Thus, the benefits resulting from the creation of insurance allow better use of scarce resources in the economy. Thanks to the use of mathematics, it is possible to adjust the amount of premiums more appropriately to the risk represented by individual insured persons. Otherwise, it would be much more difficult to determine whether a given person pays too high or too low a premium.

11 Ferguson mentions several important achievements in mathematics which, in his opinion, contributed significantly to the establishment of the insurance institution. it includes, among other things: probability (B. Pascal); collection of statistical data on deaths and births to determine the average life expectancy (J. Graunt, E. Halley); the creation of the concept of statistical significance thanks to the work of J. Bernoulli or even the work of A. de Moive on normal distribution. Interestingly, Ferguson gives 17th-century Scotland for the first time that mathematical methods were used to calculate the premium. For more information see: Ferguson (2008, pp. 187–196).

12 An underwriter is the person responsible for assessing insurance risk.

13 It can also be stated that the insurer incurs 'normal' costs not related to the use of probability, such as administrative costs, commissions paid to agents and other intermediaries, costs related to the service of insurance already concluded, etc.

14 Therefore, the names class probability, risk, and objective risk can be used interchangeably. The division into objective and subjective risks is one of many in the literature and this may lead to some semantic confusion. Subjective risk can therefore be attributed more to uncertainty.

15 It is worth mentioning that there are different types of insurance on the insurance market. For example, in the case of life insurance, a distinction is made between individual life insurance and group life insurance (usually concluded through an enterprise and partially or fully paid for by the employer). However, this division is purely technical and relates more to the institutional conditions in which the insurance contract is concluded. Of course, also in the case of individual life insurance, risk classes are created.

16 If, on the other hand, in the case of concluding a contract between two parties, the calculation of probability does not apply, it is a bet. In the case of a bet, there is a case probability.

17 Insured persons often equate health insurance with medical insurance and use these names alternately.

18 The example below is for incapacity insurance, but the same rule is true for health and medical insurance as well.

19 Randomized controlled trials (RCTs) are particularly important for insurers.

20 Therefore, life insurance was created and developed earlier than health insurance precisely because of the availability of appropriate data enabling the calculation of insurance premiums.

21 That is, the part of the premium from which the relevant benefits under the insurance contract will be paid or financed. The total premium, in turn, is the gross premium and, in addition to the net premium, it includes, inter alia, administrative costs, commission for insurance agents, or the insurer's profits.

22 It can be concluded that the more information an insurer has, the more risk groups (classes) it is able to create.

23 Therefore, the so-called cherry picking, a term often pejoratively characterizing the actions of insurers, consisting in accepting only selected risks and rejecting others, should be criticized due to the fact that it does not reflect the essence of insurance and may lead to wrong conclusions.

24 Otherwise underwriting.

25 We can distinguish two stages of risk assessment: its selection, which consists in accepting or rejecting specific risks (and persons), and risk classification, where individual insured persons are assigned to previously created risk groups (classes).

26 Another name used is negative selection.

27 It is quite a general term as there are many types of co-payment. For more on this subject see: Kozber and Osak (2013, p. 96).

28 Or, in other words, insured persons with standard risk subsidize those with sub-standard risk.

29 Such statistics should not come as a surprise, however. Here, for example, the Pareto 80/20 principle can be recalled.

30 These include, among others: concluding a contract for a specified period, e.g. for one year, introducing an appropriate level of co-payment or increasing the amount of premium or limiting the scope of insurance, if a given programme generated too high costs for the insurer. Whether the premium increase applies to the employer or employees is of secondary importance here.

31 More on word criticism: *risk transfer*, see: Michalak (2008, pp. 135–147).

32 Dealing with the calculation of insurance risk.

33 Responsible for the insurance risk assessment, e.g. by analysing applications for insurance coverage of components by potential clients of the insurer.

34 From the economic point of view, it is nothing more than a levy or tax.

35 With the help of specialized financial institutions such as banks.

References

Arrow K. J., 1971, *Essays in the theory of risk-bearing*, USA: Markham Publishing Company.

Berdine G., 2011, *The economics of US healthcare*, https://mises.org/library/economics-us-healthcare (accessed: 22. 06. 2018).

Dziełak D.et al., 2010, *Analiza korzystania ze świadczeń opieki zdrowotnej w 2009 r. i rozkładu indywidualnych wydatków Narodowego Funduszu Zdrowia związanych z finansowaniem tych świadczeń* [Analysis of the use of healthcare services in 2009 and the distribution of individual expenses of the National Health Fund related to the financing of these services], Warsaw: Centrala NFZ, Departament Świadczeń Opieki Zdrowotnej.

Ferguson F., 2008, *The ascent of money: A financial history of the world*, New York: Penguin Press.

Foss N. J., Klein P. G., 2012, *Organizing entrepreneurial judgment. A new approach to the firm*, USA: Cambridge University Press.

Guzel Z., 2013a, Organizacja i uczestnicy procesu ryzyka [Organization and participants of the risk process], in Z. Guzel, D. M. Fal, A. Lipka (eds.), *Medycyna ubezpieczeniowa: Underwritinig. Orzecznictwo. Ubezpieczenia zdrowotne* [Insurance medicine – underwriting, certification, health insurance], Warsaw: Poltext.

Guzel Z., 2013b, Ryzyko medyczne [Medical risk], in Z. Guzel, D. M. Fal, A. Lipka (eds.), *Medycyna ubezpieczeniowa: Underwritinig. Orzecznictwo. Ubezpieczenia zdrowotne* [Insurance medicine – underwriting, certification, health insurance], Warsaw: Poltext.

Hoppe H. H., 2007, The limits of numerical probability: Frank H. Knight and Ludwig von Mises and the frequency interpretation, *Quarterly Journal of Austrian Economics*, 1, 1–20.

Hoppe H. H., 2009, A four-step healthcare solution, https://mises.org/library/four-step-healthcare-solution (accessed: 22. 06. 2018).

Huber M.*et al.*, 2011, How should we define health?, *British Medical Journal*, 343, D4163.

Huerta De Soto J., 2010, *Socialism, economic calculation and entrepreneurship*, Cheltenham, Northampton: Edward Edgar Publishing.

Klimczak K. M., 2008, Ryzyko w teorii ekonomii ['Risk in economic theory'], *Master of Business Administration*, 6, 64–69.

Knight F. H., 1921, *Risk, uncertainty and profit*, New York: August M. Kelly.

Kostrzewski P., 2013, Proces oceny ryzyka w ubezpieczeniach zdrowotnych [The process of risk assessment in health insurance], in Z. Guzel, D. M. Fal, A. Lipka (eds.), *Medycyna ubezpieczeniowa: Underwritinig. Orzecznictwo. Ubezpieczenia zdrowotne/*[Insurance medicine – underwriting, certification, health insurance], Warsaw: Poltext.

Kowalewski E., 2001, Ryzyko w działalności człowieka i możliwości jego ograniczenia [The risk in human activity and the possibilities of its reduction], in T. Sangowski (ed.), *Ubezpieczenia gospodarcze [Economic insurance]*, Warsaw: Poltext.

Kozber M. M., Osak M., 2013, Współpłacenie bezpośrednie w bazowym systemie zabezpieczenia zdrowotnego – doświadczenia Szwajcarii [Direct cost sharing in the basic health system – Swiss experience], *Problemy Zarządzania*, 1, 93–111.

Light D. W., 2000, Sociological perspectives on competition in health care *Journal of Health Politics, Policy and Law*, 25, 969–974.

Lipka A., 2013a, Prawo do ubezpieczenia a prawo do oceny ryzyka. Evidence based underwriting [The right to insurance and the right to risk assessment Evidence Based Underwriting], in Z. Guzel, D. M. Fal, A. Lipka (eds.) *Medycyna ubezpieczeniowa: Underwritinig. Orzecznictwo. Ubezpieczeni zdrowotne* [Insurance medicine – underwriting, certification, health insurance], Warsaw: Poltext.

Lipka A., 2013b, Zasady oceny ryzyka w ubezpieczeniach na życie [Principles of risk assessment in life insurance], in Z. Guzel, D. M. Fal, A. Lipka (eds.), *Medycyna ubezpieczeniowa: Underwritinig. Orzecznictwo. Ubezpieczenia zdrowotne* [Insurance medicine – underwriting, certification, health insurance], Warsaw: Poltext.

Machaj M., 2013, *Kapitalizm, socjalizm i prawa własności* [Capitalism, socialism and property rights], Warsaw: Instytut Ludwiga von Misesa.

Michalak J., 2008, Przesłanki nieakceptowalności koncepcji transferu ryzyka' [Premises of unacceptability of the risk transfer concept], in J. Handschke (ed.), *Studia z ubezpieczeń gospodarczych i społecznych* [Economic and social insurance studies], Poznan: Wydawnictwo Akademii Ekonomicznej w Poznaniu, pp. 135–147.

Mises L., 1998, *Human action. A treatise on economics*, Auburn: Ludwig von Mises Institute.

Mises L., 2006, *Economic policy. Thoughts for today and tomorrow*, Auburn: Ludwig von Mises Institute.

Mises R., 1981, *Probability, statistics and truth*, USA: Courier Corporation.

Mowbray A. H., Blanchard R. H., 1961, *Insurance, its theory and practice in the United States*, New York: McGraw-Hill.

Osak M., 2008, Ryzyko zdrowotne jako podstawa wyodrębnienia ubezpieczeń zdrowotnych [Health risk as the basis for distinguishing health insurance], in J. Handschke (ed.), *Studia z ubezpieczeń gospodarczych i społecznych* [Economic and social insurance studies], Poznan: Wydawnictwo Akademii Ekonomicznej w Poznaniu, pp. 148–167.

Outerville J. F., 1998, *Theory and practice of insurance*, New York: Springer Science + Business Media.

Rockwell L. H., 2012, Freedom of association, https://mises.org/library/freedom-association (accessed: 22. 06. 2018).

Rothbard M. N., 1975, The correct theory of probability, *Libertarian Review*, 2, 9.

Rothbard M. N., 2006, *Making economic sense*, Auburn: Ludwig von Mises Institute.

Rothbard M. N., 2009, *Man, economy, and state with power and market*, Auburn: Ludwig von Mises Institute.

Sinek S., 2009, *Start with why: How great leaders inspire everyone to take action*, USA: Portfolio.

WHO, no date, What is the WHO definition of health?, http://www.who.int/suggestions/faq/en/ (accessed: 10. 06. 2018).

2 Alternative market forms of financing access to medical services

Direct payments

Direct payments (out-of-pocket) are currently not the most popular form of financing access to medical services – according to OECD data, in 2014, direct payments accounted for 15% of all expenditure on medical care among 28 European Union countries (OECD/EU, 2016, p. 123). However, they are of particular importance for decisions made by consumers. The creation and development of insurance or medical subscriptions undoubtedly allows the avoidance of a significant part of direct expenses, but this does not change the fact that these expenses are still incurred (in whole or in the majority) – in this case by the so-called third-party payer.

Direct payments are the basis of transactions in most markets. The amount of money allocated to individual goods and services is of great importance, because in the end, everything is subordinated to the judgements that consumers evaluate. Medical services are no exception in this case. The consumer is particularly attentive if they spend most of their funds on purchasing a given good or service. Their choices may turn out to be wrong at times, but they are never random. Even if they themself do not have sufficient knowledge about a given product, they often rely on the suggestions of other consumers (e.g. friends) or on the advice of specialized institutions. Price reductions and improvement in the quality of goods and services undoubtedly contribute to greater consumer satisfaction and allow producers to generate profits. However, good past performance by manufacturers is no guarantee that they will maintain their market position in the future. It depends on the ability to anticipate and meet the future needs of consumers.

Consumers allocating all or most of their funds to a given good or service cannot afford to consume them rashly, as this may worsen their situation in the future and, as a result, result in a loss for them. The

DOI: 10.4324/9781003258957-4

purchase of medical goods and services directly by the consumer should not be seen as a problem if it takes place in an unfettered market. Undistorted market competition effectively keeps costs and prices low, increases the supply and quality of the goods and services offered, and ensures their more diversified offer.

Purchasing certain goods and services has a direct impact on the rational behaviour of consumers. The situation is completely different if the consumer pays only a small fraction of the cost (as in insurance, for example). Then it is not able to fully estimate the direct cost for a given medical service, and its so-called price sensitivity is weakened or even eliminated. However, insurance contracts do not guarantee infinite access to medical services and are also subject to various types of restrictions. In health insurance contracts, the insured usually incurs part of the costs directly out of their own pocket (cost-sharing), which greatly helps insurance companies to reduce moral hazard and to keep costs and insurance premiums stable.

Currently, direct payments, which have been significantly marginalized by public healthcare, may be associated with the unpleasantness of incurring high costs, e.g. in the absence of insurance. However, in the case of problems with the availability of medical services through the so-called public health insurance is, inter alia, this form of payment that allows you to quickly access them. Importantly, thanks to direct payments, the consumer has the opportunity to purchase specific goods and services at a certain time and in the quantities they need from competing producers. There is no intermediation in the form of an insurer or a medical network. The power of the consumer making direct payments is as strong as it is in the health insurance market.

Medical savings accounts

Medical savings accounts (MSAs)[1] are also a form of direct payments. MSAs are a more institutionalized (i.e. introduced on the basis of new regulations) form of these payments, functioning within the framework of public systems, among others, in countries such as Singapore, South Africa, the United States of America, and China. Payments via MSA are made electronically (e.g. by debit card) and can be linked to health insurance as in South Africa or the USA, where the insured person pays some medical costs out of their own pocket before being able to use the insurance. In this case, the introduction of MSA made it possible to transfer funds faster or reduce the administrative costs of insurance companies.[2]

Undoubtedly, the appearance of MSA in these few countries can be read as a kind of attempt to relieve third-party payers and a step towards rationalizing the demand for medical services. One of the goals of this type of medical account is to try to influence the attitudes of consumers so that health insurance does not finance routine medical procedures that the insured can pay out of their own pocket. In addition, MSA can also affect the savings attitudes of the insured, and collecting funds for future medical (or more broadly health) expenses through a medical savings account is expected to help them in this.

The difference between MSA and regular direct payments can therefore be boiled down to the fact that in the first case, the purchase of specific medical services takes place from the funds previously accumulated for this purpose. Ordinary payments, on the other hand, may result through not purchasing other goods and services, selling some property, or voluntary savings. However, this state of affairs can be misjudged here. A person who makes a choice between saving for future medical (health) expenses and the current consumption of certain goods and services, in fact, chooses between a more or less desirable state. If such a person prefers to spend their resources on the purchase of a TV set, car, or a trip, it is a rational decision in terms of meeting urgent needs. The uncertainty of the future is not a proof of its irrational action – if it is not known what will happen in one day, and even more so in ten years, it cannot be said that current consumption (instead of saving) worsens the situation of such a person. In fact, most people can agree with the statement that having health insurance (e.g. against serious illness or accident) or saving for the so-called Black Hour is important and necessary, but it does not mean that they should all save the same amount or in the same proportion.[3] The responsibility of an individual for their own destiny is born of their freedom of choice, and only freedom of choice can teach them such responsibility to the greatest extent. For example, top-down determination of the portion of income to be allocated to MSA limits the individual's decision-making, depriving it of access to some of the funds. Therefore, an individual, after purchasing the desired goods and services (e.g. a computer), may have fewer funds that could be allocated to pro-health expenses if they had them (e.g. purchase of accessories for recreational running).

In fact, there have long been various types of medical savings accounts in the unfettered market, that is, simply savings, which did not have to be given that special name. The emergence of MSA should be considered a fairly important institutional stage of a gradual departure from financing medical services by a third party within the framework of more or less interventional public healthcare solutions. However, there are many countries where direct payments for specific medical services are made without the participation of MSA (e.g. Switzerland, the Netherlands, or Poland).

In summary, the emergence of the so-called MSA (or savings) is due to unfettered market processes enabling efficient capital accumulation and the freedom of consumer choice, and not to top-down institutional solutions. On this basis, it can be concluded that the creation and development of MSA are best served by lowering taxes and increasing tax reliefs, and not top-down regulations creating such solutions.

Medical subscriptions

Medical subscriptions as a form of indirect payments are an alternative to health insurance. Their development depends, inter alia, on institutional conditions in individual countries.

Medical networks that offer subscriptions do not, like insurance companies, assess risk with the help of insurance mathematics. Instead, they enter into contracts with doctors, nurses, and other health professionals to provide specific services within a single medical network. As a result, representatives of medical professions have a guarantee of employment and motivation to provide high-quality services. Everything is subordinated to the final consumer satisfaction. The medical subscription includes mainly outpatient services and diagnostic tests. Medical networks must therefore adequately anticipate the costs of providing such services. Unlike health insurance, the client's health does not play such a significant role. This does not mean, however, that medical networks guarantee unlimited access to medical services. Typically, when certain limits are exceeded, network customers also pay for these out of pocket. Therefore, also in the case of medical subscriptions, there are some forms of limiting the excessive consumption of medical services.

Medical networks focus on creating and developing appropriate human resources structures and procedures that enable them to generate profits with the appropriate frequency of consumption of medical services. They are first created and developed in large cities. They are favoured by a sufficiently high concentration of the population in a given area, access to qualified workers, and adequate infrastructure. These conditions favour the rapid establishment of new facilities within a given medical network.

Medical subscriptions, like health insurance, can be sold individually and in groups. In the latter form, they are often offered by employers as non-wage benefits and often compete with health insurance.

Insurance companies may, however, sign a contract for the provision of medical services to the insured with many entities, which do not have to be only medical networks. In addition, insured persons may go to other private institutions and, on the basis of presented bills, receive reimbursement up to certain amounts. On the other hand, a person with a medical subscription can usually only use the facilities of a given network.

Cooperation between medical networks and insurance companies brings benefits to both parties. Insurers do not have to incur large expenses to build their own facilities (although they can also create such a network) and can offer insured persons access to a larger number of medical facilities. On the other hand, medical networks also compete with each other for contracts with insurance companies. Thanks to such contracts, they can gain access to a wider group of clients, even if they directly lose their competition for clients with insurers. Then the insurance company monitors the quality of services provided by them on behalf of its clients. However, in the case of subscriptions, customer complaints are considered in specific medical facilities belonging to a given network. In addition, private medical networks, as a result of excessive consumption of medical services by customers, may incur higher costs than the revenues generated from subscriptions, which may result in actions on the part of the operator reducing its costs (e.g. longer waiting times and providing medical services or directing to less expensive research). In the case of group insurance, such risk may be lower, because the insurer transfers funds to a selected facility (network) as payment for medical services indicated by the insured and pays attention to their implementation, among others, at the appropriate time. Therefore, a given network which has a contract with an insurer cannot afford to extend the time of making an appointment – otherwise it may be replaced by more effective competitors.

However, medical networks will find it difficult to offer packages for relatively rare conditions that cover a small percentage of the population. In such cases, insurance companies are in a better position. In turn, medical networks will be more interested in extending their packages with medical services that can be provided to a larger group of customers – otherwise they would incur unnecessary costs.

To sum up, medical subscriptions to a certain extent both compete and complement each other with health insurance, which greatly benefits consumers (this is the case, for example, in Poland).

Charity

Charitable activity is an essential element of the market economy. Thanks to it, people who need it most can count on the help of the res-

of society, which is able to work. However, such aid is possible thanks to the constantly growing production of goods and services, which is the result of the accumulation of capital. Such a developing economy improves people's living conditions and is responsible for the increase in their welfare, which in turn contributes to the intensification of charity activities. As Mises (1998, p. 833) put it:

> Within the frame of capitalism the notion of poverty refers only to those people who are unable to take care of themselves. [...] Capitalism, in improving the masses' standard of living, hygienic conditions, and methods of prophylactics and therapeutics, does not remove bodily incapacity. It is true that today many people who in the past would have been doomed to life-long disability are restored to full vigor. But on the other hand many whom innate defects, sickness, or accidents would have extinguished sooner in earlier days survive as permanently incapacitated people. Moreover, the prolongation of the average length of life tends toward an increase in the number of the aged who are no longer able to earn a living.
>
> The problem of the incapacitated is a specific problem of human civilization and of society. [...] The very existence of a comparatively great number of invalids is, however paradoxical, a characteristic mark of civilization and material well-being.

Such conditions affect people's attitudes. Asking for help is seen more as a last resort, and people who are able to work take steps to protect themselves in the event of an uncertain future, such as taking out insurance or limiting consumption. However, this is not an effect of dependence on the ruthless capitalist system, but actions that testify to their freedom of choice and independence. Units with insurance policies, their own savings, and other forms of protection in the event of uncertain events (e.g. accidents or diseases) do not constitute an economic burden for the rest of society. Through appropriate market institutions (commercial and non-commercial) they are able to take care of themselves. This state of affairs in the 1920s was well captured by American president C. Coolidge, who stated that 'There is no dignity quite so impressive and no independence quite so important as living within your means' (Maxwell, 2003, p. 101). This statement clearly contrasts with the contemporary calls of many politicians to increase the role of the state in providing society with the so-called social security.

It is important in this case that various market solutions create appropriate structures for financing access to medical services. Thanks to this, people involved in the production process have greater safety and can allocate part of their own resources to helping people in need. From the economic perspective, there are two basic conditions for providing assistance to those in need: the availability of appropriate resources and the will. People who voluntarily donate funds to those in need value the satisfaction with providing them higher than the preservation of these funds or their consumption. The benefits they obtain are therefore not of a monetary nature. Willingness to improve someone's situation motivates to action and gives a sense of satisfaction. Whether such an action is motivated by religious considerations, internal sensitivity to human harm, or other motives does not matter for the economy – the act of action itself and its effects count.

Even in modern economies, subject to many interventions damaging market productivity, one can observe an endless variety of charitable actions, on either an ad hoc or permanent (institutional) nature. Among other things, thanks to the development of the Internet, relatively quick collections of multi-million sums are possible. Such expenses are associated with the purchase of expensive drugs and/or the financing of expensive therapies, i.e. medical goods and services that are only affordable for very wealthy people. However, charity allows us to overcome this barrier, because in this case the founder is thousands of people providing support – even the most modest one. This has another positive effect. The additional demand for rare and expensive medical services encourages manufacturers to produce them more efficiently. The demand for these types of innovative and, in a sense, luxury goods and services no longer comes from only the highest-income people, which gives hope for their faster mass production in the future. Thanks to charity work, people with medium or low income also indirectly participate in setting trends or directions for the development of innovative medical goods and services.

An important feature of charity activity is its directness and informality. People who show such support are guided to a large extent by emotional criteria, which has many advantages. The situation is different in the case of various public programmes (non-market, non-charity), where there are clearly defined procedures. The sensitivity and good will of the donor is replaced by a formalized clerical decision leading to top-down selection of who is eligible for such assistance and who is not, which is a distortion of the act of providing assistance.

It is also important that market solutions enable the development of many charity institutions that improve these processes by quickly directing the attention of society to the cases of people most in need of support and by obtaining the necessary funds to improve their situation. In addition, thanks to such activity, the supporters also develop appropriate ethical attitudes and, at least indirectly, contribute to their promotion among the rest of society.

Notes

1 Another name used is health savings accounts (HSAs).
2 For more on the principles of MSA operation in selected countries, see: Goodman et al. (2004, pp. 110–111, 135–137).
3 This is due, inter alia, to the wide variety of needs for certain medical services – consumers do not report demand for one type of healthcare.

References

Goodman J. C., Musgrave G. L., Herrick D. M., 2004, *Lives at risk. Single-payer national health insurance around the world*, USA: Rowman & Littlefield Publishers.

Maxwell J. C., 2003, *There's no such thing as 'business' ethics: There's only one rule for making decisions*, USA: Warner Books.

Mises L., 1998, *Human action. A treatise on economics*, Auburn: Ludwig von Mises Institute.

OECD/EU, 2016, *Health at a glance: Europe 2016 – state of health in the EU cycle*, Paris: OECD Publishing.

3 The health system as an element of the market economy

Relationships between the various forms of financing access to medical services

When considering the functioning of market solutions in the field of providing consumers with medical (or health-related) goods and services, first of all, one should consider their appropriate definition. However, instead of describing these processes as market or private healthcare (as an alternative to public healthcare), it is more appropriate to use terms such as the private or market health system and the universal (public) health system.[1]

The very word 'healthcare' is very generalized and fuzzy. There is often talk of the need for people to have access to healthcare by the state, but there are no cases of countries having identical healthcare systems – on the contrary, there is a wide variety of them. However, healthcare is viewed as some kind of abstract, unified good that everyone needs. However, in reality no one consumes more or less units of the general healthcare resource. It is also confusing to talk about the so-called right to healthcare. It is not a right to use one homogeneous good. People differ both physiologically and psychologically. Additionally, they participate in random events causing undesirable effects (e.g. accidents or diseases). In fact, a person does not report a demand for healthcare in general, but for specific medical goods and services (or more broadly health services) aimed at reducing or eliminating their discomfort. The market (manufacturers) is thus responsible for meeting these diverse consumer health needs by providing heterogeneous goods and services, rather than one universal product under the misleading name of healthcare.[2]

The use of the term health system instead of the healthcare system has important economic and praxeological justification. Many people agree that if you get sick or have an accident, you should get treatment

DOI: 10.4324/9781003258957-5

as soon as possible. However, this intuitive agreement does not mean that they perceive these threats in the same way and take identical actions to prevent them. Contrary to popular belief, health does not have to be the most important thing – a lot depends on the human situation. For example, it is difficult to expect that young and unhealthy people will undergo thorough examinations every quarter or be interested in having a wide range of health insurance. Thus, they do not necessarily have to be willing to engage in this type of action. The situation is different in the case of people who are already ill – for them health will be ranked higher or highest in their hierarchy of needs. There is no rigid division or classification of needs here – everything depends on the judgements that value consumers and producers try to follow these needs. Therefore, a health need should be considered undergoing a complicated surgery, consultations, and examinations with a specialist doctor, taking medications as well as purchasing a gym ticket, walking in the forest, changing the diet, or going to bed earlier. Each individual meets their needs with the help of preselected means. So, they create their own plan or system to do this. Their needs are specific and often require the involvement of a set of complementary measures. Such a situation results in the emergence of specific complex market structures, reflecting decisions made by consumers.

Contrary to the universal (public) health system, its market counterpart does not have a single, institutionalized, rigid structure. The framework of the market system is not predetermined and is constantly changing. The health system, as an important part of the market economy, functions on the same principles as its other elements (markets). Perhaps due to the lack of this fixed 'shape' (or difficulties in defining it) the market health system may seem to be a less attractive solution than the public system. However, for economics and the economy, not only are the dynamics of market processes or their diversity important, but also the study of the effects that these processes bring. The market is not an abstract, changing entity that consumers must constantly adapt to. The market is the result of their actions. The essence of the market was well reflected by Mises (1998, p. 270):

> The market is not a place, a thing, or a collective entity. The market is a process, actuated by the interplay of the actions of the various individuals cooperating under the division of labor. The forces determining the – continually changing – state of the market are the value judgments of these individuals and their actions as directed by these value judgments. The state of the market at any instant is the price structure, i.e., the totality of the exchange ratios

as established by the interaction of those eager to buy and those eager to sell. There is nothing inhuman or mystical with regard to the market. The market process is entirely a resultant of human actions. Every market phenomenon can be traced back to definite choices of the members of the market society.

[...]

The direction of all economic affairs is in the market society a task of the entrepreneurs. Theirs is the control of production. They are at the helm and steer the ship. A superficial observer would believe that they are supreme. But they are not. They are bound to obey unconditionally the captain's orders. The captain is the consumer. Neither the entrepreneurs nor the farmers nor the capitalists determine what has to be produced. The consumers do that. If a businessman does not strictly obey the orders of the public as they are conveyed to him by the structure of market prices, he suffers losses, he goes bankrupt, and is thus removed from his eminent position at the helm. Other men who did better in satisfying the demand of the consumers replace him.

Although the entire production process is ultimately subordinated to consumers, they mainly come into contact only with producers of final goods and services. The so-called higher stages of production, although not of their interest, are also subordinate economically to them. The changes taking place there affect the final shape of the market only if consumers accept them.

This is one of the reasons why health insurance plays such an important role in the market health system. Due to reliable risk assessment of insurance companies, when the need arises, they are able to provide access to specific medical services under the previously indicated conditions. The fact that health insurance is not the only market form of financing access to such services is due to at least four reasons. First of all, health insurance has its limitations in financing access to these services – it does not guarantee unlimited access. Insurance companies try to limit the moral hazard in order not to increase premiums exceeding the expectations of the insured. Insured persons paying a fraction of the cost may use certain services much more often than if they incurred the costs directly. Secondly, not all events are insurable, that is, not all events can be accounted for in an economic calculation based on probability, and thus prices (premiums) can be determined. Third, not every person must feel the same need to adequately protect themselves against the adverse effects of losing health. Some people prefer to allocate their funds to other goods or services and, in the event of an accident or illness, pay e.g. directly for certain medical services. Fourthly, there may be substitutes for health insurance on the market, e.g. in the form of medical subscriptions, which to some extent offer access to the same medical services.

Moreover, it should also be emphasized that while insurance, to a certain extent, allows for relief from the burden of significant health expenses, their development should not be directly equated with the growing production of medical goods and services. The constantly growing demand for this type of good and service may be generated both by third-party payers (insurance companies, medical networks, and charities) and individual consumers (direct payments). One can imagine a situation where the production of such goods and services does not change or declines, but the demand generated by the growing number of insured continues to grow. In such a situation, premiums will also increase. The allocation of a fraction of the costs by the insured is possible thanks to the actions of insurance companies and the processes of competition. However, paying 10% of the cost in the form of an insurance premium, for example, does not result from a tenfold increase in supply, which is something to keep in mind. Falling health insurance prices may have their source both in the growing quality of risk assessment and in the ever-increasing supply of needed medical goods and services, but without this growing supply (and medical knowledge), the health insurance market would have very limited growth prospects despite the advances in insurance mathematics.

One can agree with the view that having health insurance or a medical subscription gives great comfort and these services/forms of payment may be of the greatest interest to consumers. However, direct payments will continue to play an equally important (or even fundamental) role in the market health system. Thanks to them, the consumer can easily estimate the cost of a given service, which affects the rationality of their decisions. The price system makes it easy for every consumer to find out about a given situation and make a decision about the amount of consumption. A consumer paying out-of-pocket will not be mismanaged. Direct payments are therefore a kind of anchor influencing the rational choices of the consumer and are a good alternative in the absence of insurance or medical subscription. As was mentioned before, nowadays they may be associated with incurring high costs, but this is the result of more interventions than in other markets. In addition, direct payments also allow for the development of innovation in the field of medical services, thanks to which specialized institutions providing innovative solutions are created. As indicated by Goodman et al. (2004, p. 248):

What Harvard University professor Regina Herzlinger calls 'focused factories,' providing highly efficient, specialized care, are becoming a reality. These health care businesses deliver lower prices, lower mortality rates, shorter stays and higher patient satisfaction.

For example, the Johns Hopkins Breast Center is a focused factory for mastectomies. The Dartmouth-Hitchcock Medical Center in Lebanon, New Hampshire, is a focused factory for heart surgery. The Pediatrix Medical Group, which manages neonatal units and provides pediatric services in twenty-one states, is another example. Focused factories also are cropping up around the country to provide cancer, gynecological and orthopedic services. One spectacular success story is Dr. Bernard Salick, a kidney specialist who has become a millionaire by pioneering a national chain of round-the-clock cancer clinics.

Insurance companies also often cooperate with many 'focused factories' by creating new insurance products, e.g. enabling coverage of significant costs of treatment (e.g. cancer) in highly specialized institutions operating in different countries. These 'focused factories' are therefore provided with an additional source of income. Despite the high sums insured, the premiums are not unattainable for the majority of those interested, inter alia, thanks to the creation of global, transnational risk groups by insurance companies. The greater the number of insured persons (and the available data), the easier it is to reliably assess and monitor the risk. Thanks to this, when, for example, an insured person, a Polish citizen, is diagnosed with a serious illness falling within the scope of such insurance, in the economic sense, their treatment in a specialized institution is in fact financed by the insured from all over the world. This is a good example of how entrepreneurial processes give people around the world the chance to better secure an uncertain future without them interacting directly. Tourist insurance that covers the costs of treatment abroad or medical tourism, which allows access to certain medical services outside the country's borders, also play an equally useful role. These examples show that a market-based healthcare system, at least in part, can be global in scope.

In addition, insurance companies or medical networks can also stimulate the development of the drug market, medical services, or medical equipment. Undoubtedly, insurers have an interest in ensuring that their clients enjoy good health as long as possible – this results in lower consumption of insurance and allows for a reduction in premiums. Taking 'uncertain' medications or using the services of 'uncertain' doctors may worsen the health of the insured person and, as a result lead to more frequent use of health insurance. Of course, in a market-based healthcare system, there would be no compulsory licences required by public institutions. However, this does not mean that the licensing system would not function at all. On the contrary, a system of licences issued by competing institutions, such as associations of doctors, pharmacists, and other medical professionals, would be an excellent competitive advantage. Drug manufacturers or young, novice doctors would seek licences issued by various institutions, as these would increase their competitiveness.[3] In turn, the institutions issuing them would scrupulously evaluate the persons or enterprises applying for them for their products, because otherwise they would quickly fall out of the market, and their place would be taken by more reliable institutions. In an uninterrupted market where the consumer's power is not limited, the loss of consumer confidence has very serious consequences. Therefore, building consumer confidence in specific institutions or a given brand is gaining importance. This is also one of the reasons why insurance companies would be interested in their own activity in such markets, as they could have a greater impact on limiting health risk. If the insured would use the services of doctors recommended by insurance companies or take safe drugs, they would have a positive effect on their health. As a result, insurance companies could further develop the system of insurance discounts granted for the use of appropriate quality medical goods and services or even for active actions of the insured reducing the probability of disease or accidents (Tannenhill & Tannenhill, 2009, pp. 50–51). The insured persons could therefore lead a more active lifestyle which, if properly documented, would entitle them to receive a discount.

Insurance companies would thus contribute to the systematic improvement of the quality of medical goods and services, e.g. by holding shares in pharmaceutical companies or companies producing medical equipment. It can also be assumed that they would be very interested in supporting small, but innovative enterprises, which they would help in management and provide capital support. Such analysis shows the great potential of unrestricted market processes that do not create a rigid framework, but are constantly transformed, which benefits consumers – the final beneficiaries of the effects of these changes.

However, even in a private health system, it should be taken into account that the costs of financing access to medical services for a certain part of the society may turn out to be too high. On the one hand, people are not perfect and make mistakes, and on the other hand, it is very difficult to predict all possible developments in the future. These inconveniences can be (and are) effectively limited or eliminated by broadly understood charitable activities. Thanks to this type of activity, it is possible to overcome situations when basic forms of financing access to health services are not able to provide such access. An example is an extremely rare disease that is not insurable and, in addition, is very expensive to treat. In such situations, neither insurance nor medical subscription will help. The only option, there-fore, is to finance expensive treatment in a specialized unit through the good will of other people. This may raise some concerns; for some, such application for help may even be considered derogatory – the lack of insurance or sufficient resources leads to a situation where it is necessary to turn to the last resort in the form of asking for help. However, insurance is also a kind of form of helping some people over others. The rules on which this support is provided are set by insurance companies, playing the role of agents caring for the interests of their clients. It should also be noted that the existence of predetermined solutions may not always be beneficial. If the subjects of support for charitable activities are rare, difficult cases, as well as those which give little chance of success, then establishing rigid rules of functioning for them will not be beneficial either for the helpers or for those who need this help. On what basis should it be determined in advance who is to help who and how much? That is why, thanks to various spontaneous initiatives and charitable institutions specializing in this type of activ-ity, it is possible to provide the necessary support in a very short time. The greatest potential and at the same time value in this type of activity lies in the understanding that charity is an indispensable ele-ment of the market health system, and not just an unpleasant addition. Due to the fact that, in principle, every person can suffer great mis-fortune at any time, it is a rational and economic justification for society to direct its help to people who need it most.

   An equally important effect of the market health system is the growing responsibility of individuals for their fate, which is why they will treat all kinds of charity as a last resort, and people who raise doubts about receiving this type of help will be carefully verified by charity institutions. Thanks to this type of action, society will become more aware that people who receive help really need it. An additional positive effect will also be the development of appropriate ethical atti-tudes in the society. Maxwell (2003, pp. 23–24), referring to the Josephson Institute of Ethics, draws attention to the existence of two dimensions of ethics:

> The first involves the ability to discern right from wrong, good from evil, and propriety from impropriety. The second involves the

commitment to do what is right, good and proper. Ethics entails action; it is not just a topic to mull or debate.

At this point, it is worth paying attention to the important role played by the family institution in the market health system. Humans are beings who have recognized the benefits of the division of labour. Thanks to the existence of society, it is easier to meet your needs and the first social substitute in the life of every human being is the family. Therefore, in the discussion on the functioning of the market healthcare system, it should be noted that in a situation requiring support from the rest of the society, before this support occurs, the first costs and assistance are often already provided by members of the immediate or extended family. Therefore, the person needing help is not placed between their own decisions (e.g. paying for insurance or subscription fees or collecting savings) and the help of third parties. On this basis, charity work can be considered as a kind of extension of help from a neighbour to the rest of society. Also, therefore, family packages in the form of health insurance or subscriptions play an important role on the market. You can also see the benefits of using a medical savings account by one, previously authorized, family member in emergency situations, e.g. when such a person needs to urgently use an ambulance service.

The market health system and so-called market failures

When describing the aspects of the functioning of the market health system, one should also refer to the so-called market failures. The most important of these are the problem of asymmetric information, healthcare as a public good, and the possibility of the formation of monopolies on the markets. These market defects are intended to prevent the effective provision of medical goods and services needed by the society on market terms and to justify the necessary state intervention.

Asymmetric information

In the case of the asymmetric information as a source of market failure, the arguments contained in the works of Kenneth J. Arrow (1963, pp. 941–973) and G. A. Akerlof (1970, pp. 488–500) should be analysed. Although they were established some time ago, they still form the basis of arguments against health market solutions. For example, it is believed that Arrow's article had a great influence on the creation of the so-called health economics and the development of other research areas such as public choice theory, sociology, banking, and education.[4]

It is also worth emphasizing that in 1963 the state's interference in the market healthcare system was much smaller than it is now, where third-party payers with public programmes such as Medicare or Medicaid (Savedoff, 2004, pp. 139–140) (in the case of the USA) dominate, and the content presented by Arrow was undoubtedly intellectual argument for introducing these programmes in 1965.

Treatment of the so-called asymmetric information as an alleged market failure is problematic for several reasons. Firstly, the mere fact that one of the parties to the transaction (usually the seller) has more information about the product or service does not necessarily mean that the other party (the buyer) will be cheated and receive a product that does not meet their expectations. To put it differently, the existence of asymmetric information does not have to and usually has no negative economic consequences. The very term asymmetry has an element of value and a pejorative overtone. Meanwhile, this disproportion in knowledge is nothing more than a differently defined division of knowledge and labour in the economy that enables trade and the development of markets. Asymmetric information results, among other things, from the fact that people have different skills, which results in a division of labour and a constantly deepening specialization. Also, natural conditions, such as the presence of raw materials, are not the same for the entire world. Moreover, even if it were possible to imagine a situation in which people have the same (in place and time) access to information, it does not solve the problem in any way, because they can interpret it differently and on this basis take different actions (DiLorenzo, 2011, pp. 250–252). People do not function as predetermined algorithms or calculators, to which it is enough to enter the same data to give the same results. The same information does not imply the same actions or effects.[5]

Secondly, it is true that deepening knowledge, specialization, and the emergence of new professions lead to ever greater information disproportions, but this does not amount to unfair treatment of clients. If the assumptions about the asymmetric information were reduced to their logical consequences, producers would only achieve such benefits at the beginning, and then markets would experience stagnation. The shortcomings of the products would become apparent after a while. Competitive advantage would therefore have to rely on increasingly sophisticated ways of concealing information from naive customers who do not draw conclusions from defective products. In reality, however, the fact that the seller has more information about the product or service than the buyer does is more of a kind of problem for them, and certainly a challenge to best close this gap. The goal of any exchange i for both sides of the transaction to make a profit, i.e. a situation in which the benefits of the exchange exceed its costs. On the part of producers, this determines activities aimed at highlighting the benefits that buyers can bring to the purchase of a given good or service. To achieve this goal, they must not only offer a product of the right quality and price, but also dispel customer doubts arising from the lack of information that interests them, which in turn increases uncertainty. In market conditions, one of the sources of competitive advantage may be appropriate customer relations, such as providing information on the usefulness of the product or after-sales service. If the manufacturer can gain a competitive advantage thanks to this, it will be easier if the competitors' products have defects that they try to hide from customers.

Third, economists describing the alleged market failure in the form of asymmetric information do not seem to pay sufficient attention to how markets deal with this asymmetry. For example, Akerlof argues that manufacturers offering low-quality cars (so-called lemons) would become dominant in the used car market, as they would have more information about the goods sold. He did not notice, however, that at the time of the publication of his work, there were 30-day guarantees on the used car market. Continuing this line of reasoning, such a market should collapse, and at the same time, nothing like that has happened and is not happening. One might also wonder why similar practices of unfair sellers should only be carried out on the secondary market. Car manufacturers also have an information advantage, but the quality of their products and the state of the market do not confirm the predictions of Akerlof. Both on the primary and secondary market there is competition, insurance, guarantees, numerous advisory institutions, and knowledge resources in the form of internet portals evaluating both sellers and buyers. As Berdine (2017a, p. 66) points out:

> The market solution to information asymmetry is the market for asymmetric information. Experts sell advice. Advice that changes a decision to purchase something very costly is very valuable. The market solves the problem of information asymmetry by selling the advice for a much lower price than the price of the decision to be made.

All these solutions are aimed at meeting the needs of customers, including their demand for information. Both sellers and buyers are not omniscient and can make mistakes, but one of the advantages of market solutions is that they are quickly exposed through the profit and loss mechanism.

Another example of market failure caused by asymmetric information is the health insurance market. The person applying for insurance knows their health well and is better able to assess the risk of falling ill than the insurer. Moreover, they may deliberately not disclose the key information from the perspective of the insurance risk assessment in the medical questionnaire in order to obtain a lower premium or be covered by a given insurance programme at all. Such a situation means that people with a higher health risk than those with a lower risk are interested in joining the insurance. This phenomenon is called anti-selection. If such persons are insured (e.g. on standard terms instead of sub-standard terms), the costs will exceed income and an increase in premiums will be needed to cover this disproportion. This will lead to the resignation of some insured persons with lower health risk and there will be another increase. This process is known as the death spiral (Morris et al., 2012, p. 141). It is also interesting that in this case it is the insured (buyer) who has the advantage over the insurer (seller) and not the other way around.

However, such a presentation of the case would mean that insurance companies are not able to accurately assess insurance risk, which is in fact the core of their business. If insurance companies are unable to make an appropriate selection and classification of the insured, they suffer losses and give way to competitors. Moreover, it would be extremely naive to argue that these institutions are at the mercy of the ethical behaviour of insured persons. In fact, insurers have developed a number of solutions to properly assess and verify the insurance risk. These include, among others: medical surveys and examinations, access to information on the health condition of the insured person from various sources prior to the conclusion of insurance, exclusions and limitations of the scope of insurance cover, grace periods, or concluding fixed-term contracts. The use of the above tools along with the development of insurance mathematics has led to the development of the health insurance market, not its stagnation. Many diseases that were previously uninsurable or unknown are today in the field of health insurance. It is true that insurance companies are struggling with dishonesty and moral hazard on the part of the insured, but these are not problems that herald the collapse of this market. Insurers should be left free to act.

Interestingly, Arrow believes that the lack of many risks in health insurance and medical care services proves a market failure and if the market cannot provide health insurance to the whole society then the state should do so (Berdine, 2016, p. 60). This view should be criticized for two reasons. First of all, as has already been mentioned, the health insurance market is constantly developing and since 1963 it has been easy to see its progress, which is possible, among others, thanks to the development of medicine and the processes of competition. Second, you may agree that it is not possible to insure everyone against everything, but that is not evidence of an insurance market failure. For Arrow, the lack of insurance coverage is equated with market failure in general. Therefore, it should be emphasized once again that insurance is one of the forms of financing access to medical services, and the basis is direct payments, as is the case in many other markets: food, transport, computer, etc. The insurance institution allows you to free yourself from a part of significant health expenses but does not guarantee unlimited funding opportunities. Not all events are insurable or insured. The inability to perform an economic calculation based on probability does not necessarily have to be seen as a market flaw – if the premium (insurance price) cannot be rationally determined, then there is no basis for the economic use of scarce resources in the economy. That is why direct payments (and other forms of financing) are so important, because thanks to them the society easily receives information about the availability of rare goods and services through the price structure.

Public goods

Arguments for the existence of asymmetric information lead supporters of public healthcare to conclude that it is a special good, different from other goods and services provided under market conditions. On the one hand, there is a risk that the consumer (patient) will not be able to adequately assess the quality of goods and services, and sellers will use this situation to increase their profits. On the other hand, a lack of proper knowledge may turn against them and they may also take a light-hearted approach to, for example, buying insurance or paying for an examination that can detect a serious illness. Therefore, the only way out of this stalemate is state intervention to replace the flawed market solutions. The means for this is the creation of one (or more) public health programmes. It may be defined as public healthcare or otherwise, however, the principles of its operation and financing are predetermined by the state. It can then be concluded that a number of heterogeneous medical (health) goods and services with an appropriate price structure are replaced by public healthcare and treated as the so-called public good.

In this study, less technical (and rigorous) and earlier than Samuelson's, definition of a public good as a good produced by the state (government) and generally available for the benefit of its citizens was adopted. A more technical definition by Samuelson treats a public good as a good that, once produced for some consumers, can be consumed by others without additional, marginal costs of such consumption (the so-called non-competition in consumption) (Holcombe, 2007, pp. 2–3). The reference to a more general definition can be justified by the fact that the process of creating public healthcare systems or social welfare systems by states started at the end of the 19th century (Germany), i.e. before the publication of Samuelson's (1954, pp. 387–389) article in 1954. Also, earlier during World War II, Great Britain, on the basis of a Beveridge report, began to create a public healthcare system (National Health Service) which started operating in 1948. Public health systems became popular after the Second World War, and by 1949 they were already functioning in 36 countries (Monkiewicz, 2002, p. 388). Moreover, Samuelson cited national defence or lighthouses as classic examples of public goods. From the point of view of the Austrian School, one can agree as to the presence of goods with the characteristics indicated by Samuelson,[6] but this fact does not prevent their delivery on market principles (Kwiatkowski, 2010, p. 110).

For example, the use of private medical consultations and tests provides information about the patient's health and allows for earlier detection of the disease. So, the risk of infecting others with it decreases. Moreover, such a person, e.g. a company director, may not get sick at all or experience milder symptoms and return to work faster, which is related to its better functioning. The presence of the director means that important decisions can still be made on an ongoing basis. The company does not experience downtime resulting in delayed deliveries. Similar external benefits are shared by insurance companies, medical networks, and charities, and while they may differ, this does not in any way negate the fact that private institutions generate them.[7]

The need to provide society with a universal healthcare system may also be argued with equity or income criteria. The wealthier or less needy part of society should support the more needy. People should be sure that they will not be deprived of support in the event of illness or accident. It is believed that the state, through its activity in the area of healthcare, provides society with the so-called right to healthcare. However, the present meaning of the term has a strongly interventionist meaning.

In the conditions of voluntary relationships taking place on the market, the phrase having the right to something means a situation in which an individual has a choice that no one can (has the right) to impose on them by force, and they themself cannot use it to achieve their goals at the expense of other members of society. For example the right to own a house or apartment means that a person can choose any offer from among those available on the market, guided by their own needs and financial possibilities. They have the right to decide how they will meet their housing needs. They are not condemned to the mercy of sellers, as they are also a seller in another industry, e.g. automotive, where the general principles of success are the same – customer satisfaction. The right to a house or flat of such a person will be limited, for example, when restrictive building regulations limiting the supply of houses and flats come into force or when higher taxes are passed to finance military operations. The principle is the same for healthcare. The right to healthcare means that a person has the choice between different, competing providers offering the goods and medical services they need. Its law materializes both when concluding such transactions and when refraining from them. The prices of certain goods and services that are too high for such a person do not deprive that person of the right to them, but only testify to their low availability and at the same time constitute an incentive for other entrepreneurs to produce cheaper, but adequately quality products. Examples of limiting this right include, for example, regulations limiting the supply of doctors, medical equipment, or drugs, which give the consumer a smaller choice. The modern right to healthcare means consent to forcing the greater part of society to provide it to others,[8] and any plans to limit state intervention in this area are treated as attempts to limit or deprive society of previously acquired privileges or the right to healthcare.

The modern right to healthcare cannot guarantee unlimited access to medical services, as the means of implementing this right are of an economic nature, that is, they are limited. By juxtaposing these limitations with the lack of market incentives to establish appropriate supply-demand relations, everyone (or a certain part of society) will try to exercise their rights in a world of limited resources without being fully aware of it. However, the lack of an adequate pricing structure, coupled with the ever-increasing demand, which stems from the right to healthcare, will be one of the main reasons why this target cannot be achieved. In the growing demand for financing medical services by the state, providers of these services will also benefit from their benefits, as they can thus guarantee a constant (non-market) demand for their services and limit competition through a dense network of regulations, requirements, and licences. In such circumstances, the constantly increasing costs must ultimately lead to limitations in access to healthcare. Society will see an increase in contributions and/or taxes and hence expenditure, which is an inherent feature of public health systems. If society accepts the higher costs, it will not be possible to pretend that the right to healthcare is cost-free – that is, the ever-increasing demand has economic consequences. This will be a non-market signal of resource constraints. An alternative is to introduce smaller or larger restrictions on access to healthcare, which may take various forms and names: cost (budget) control, queues to doctors, or extending waiting times for an appointment to the doctor or surgery. These various forms of rationing also show resource scarcity. What's important, however, is that their introduction essentially contradicts the fundamental assumption of unlimited right (and access) to healthcare – because it limits access to what, by definition, should be unlimited (Berdine, 2017b, pp. 25–26).

The above arguments also show that even taking into account Samuelson's definition of public goods, marginal (additional) costs are actually generated by public systems and also include those consumers who, by theoretical assumption, were not supposed to pay them at all. It is also visible in practice, as premiums paid by healthier and/ or professionally active insured persons are not able to adequately ensure access to medical services to all beneficiaries – hence the increase in the amount of premiums or regulation of services covering all insured persons. This is basically the case in all developed countries where people of retirement age, in an economic sense, do not bear any financial cost of health insurance. However, they bear other costs, e.g. in the form of longer queues to the doctor, a decrease in the quality of services, etc. This rationing is therefore a different form or reaction to the appearance of competition in the consumption of these services, i.e. a phenomenon that the definition and essence of public goods formulated by Samuelson had excluded.[9]

Moreover, even if some insured persons benefit at the initial stage – e.g. subsidized persons – this happens at the expense of groups with lower health risk, which, in order to avoid queues, may decide, for example, to purchase additional private insurance, etc.

In the discussion on the functioning of modern healthcare systems, too little attention is paid to possible market alternatives. The current shape of constantly expanded public systems, various forms of rationing, or constantly growing costs reflect well the consequences of abandoning rational market solutions. The market healthcare system is not able to use a magic wand to turn scarce resources into limitless ones, but thanks to human creativity and the processes of competition, it is able to increase the quantity and quality of the goods and services needed.

Monopolies

While the main arguments against market solutions focus primarily on asymmetric information or the perception of healthcare as a public good, there are also issues of monopoly formation in unfettered markets. The very concept of monopoly is not precise, however, and there are also some differences between the economists of the Austrian School.[10] In this study, the definition of Rothbard (2009, p. 669) was adopted, indicating (and justifying it accordingly) that:

> monopoly is a grant of special privilege by the State, reserving a certain area of production to one particular individual or group. Entry into the field is prohibited to others and this prohibition is enforced by the gendarmes of the State.

This definition is therefore closely related to interventionism. Other definitions of monopoly (or monopoly) as the sole seller of a given good, or the person to obtain the monopoly price, were thoroughly criticized by Rothbard.[11]

In this sense, on an unhampered market, monopolies do not arise, but properly functioning market structures or entities that better satisfy consumers' needs than competitors. They owe their dominant position or monopoly only to better anticipation of future market conditions. The consumer making their choice is not guided by sentiment, and if a new product that better meets their needs appears on the market, then the merits of the former producers do not matter. If a manufacturer is still trusted by customers and has achieved its position in the market through voluntary exchanges, there is no threat of a monopoly. Any market price is fair in the sense that it is determined by the sovereign decisions of buyers and sellers. Demanding state intervention to break up such a monopoly would be highly uneconomical, as part of the capital would go to entities that are not so well able to meet the needs of consumers, which would result in incurring losses and wasting capital.

The purpose of the market is not for countless small players to function. The market does not protect the big companies or exalt the small ones.[12] They are all subject to the same rules – in this sense, they have equal opportunities.

The arguments that representatives of the medical industry, for example doctors, can obtain very high prices or monopoly prices, demanding exorbitant amounts for treatment from sick patients, should also be considered untrue. The salary of a doctor or any other representative of the medical or health industry depends on the quality of their work (customer satisfaction) and competition. This was well presented by Mises (1998, p. 660):

> What produces a man's profit in the course of affairs within an unhampered market society is not his fellow citizen's plight and distress, but the fact that he alleviates or entirely removes what causes his fellow citizen's feeling of uneasiness. What hurts the sick is the plague, not the physician who treats the disease. The doctor's gain is not an outcome of the epidemics, but of the aid he gives to those affected.

Moreover, public health systems and private entities cooperating with them are much closer to the monopoly position. In this case, the consumer cannot choose the supplier. Regulations concerning manufacturers of drugs, medical equipment, or medical professions are above the power of the consumer, although they are introduced in the consumer's interest.

In this context, it is also worth paying attention to the issue of the so-called natural monopoly, which was supposed to mean a situation in which, among others, due to the substantial or massive scale of production, the producer concerned may have achieved a total unit cost lower than it would have been if there had been two or more competitors in the market. Thus, a single entity was to be more effective, which at the same time was to serve as a justification for granting it special privileges by the state. In this case, the existence of more entities would be ineffective and, paradoxically, would lead to higher prices. For example, in the history of the USA (at the turn of the 19th and 20th centuries), the recognition of a given enterprise as the so-called the natural monopolist was also seen as a way of restricting competition in a non-market manner (DiLorenzo, 1996, p. 43).

The economists of the Austrian School point out that the processes of competition are dynamic, which may lead to the existence of many competitors in a given market and several or even one entity. However, even the latter situation is not indicative of market failure. Such an entrepreneur could have achieved their position at any given moment by, for example, achieving the lowest costs, efficient management, and better anticipation of consumer needs. However, the success of the sole manufacturer attracts the attention of potential competitors that could quickly become real competitors (DiLorenzo, 1996, p. 44). Even if this does not happen, the current market leader must constantly develop its business if it does not want to go out of the market or significantly lose its position over time – it does not even have to be the result of the existence of many competitors, but the possibility of their appearance. That is why the lack of governmental regulations restricting these processes is so important.

Also, mergers, acquisitions, and trusts do not pose a threat to free competition and consumers. On the contrary, they testify to high capital accumulation and efficient management leading to lower prices. These processes also do not eliminate smaller entities, but integrate them into their own structures, while increasing their efficiency. For example, American trusts from the late 19th century, thanks to the scale of their operations, were able to increase production and lower prices faster than the rest of the economy.[13]

Standard Oil, developed and developed by J. D. Rockefeller, is a good example here. In 1899, Standard Oil refined 90% of the US crude oil. However, this did not translate into higher oil prices due to the company's use of its monopoly position. On the contrary, both refining costs and retail oil prices have been steadily falling. The latter fell to their lowest levels in history in 1897 – to 5.91 cents a barrel – at a time when Standard Oil had the largest market share (Reed, 2015, pp. 338, 343).

Many believed that such significant size and market share would lead to monopoly pricing. However, as Reed (2015, p. 353) points out:

> According to the notion that Standard's size gave it the power to charge any price, bigness per se immunizes the firm from competition and consumer sovereignty.
>
> As an 'efficiency monopoly,' Standard could not coercively prevent others from competing with it. And others did, so much so that the company's share of the market declined dramatically after 1899. As the economy shifted from kerosene to electricity, from the horse to the automobile, and from oil production in the East to production in the Gulf States, Rockefeller found himself losing ground to younger, more aggressive competitors.
>
> Neither did Standard have the power to compel people to buy its products.It had to rely on its own excellence to attract and keep customers.

This proves both the lack of establishing the so-called monopoly prices by entities with the largest market shares, as well as the fact that the potential recognition of Standard Oil as a natural monopoly would limit dynamic competition processes, which over time led to a decline in its market share, but continued to adequately satisfy the needs of consumers.

Notes

1 The justification for the use of the term 'universal health system' is described in more detail on pp. 00–00.
2 See also a comment by Prof. P. Klein (2013) on the definition of healthcare.
3 For example, medical networks could recruit only doctors with qualifications confirmed by appropriate certificates.
4 In this case, the authority or influence of Arrow can be compared, for example, to the authority of J. S. Mill, who in the 19th century argued for the introduction of public education, which resulted in the Education Act.
5 Moreover, eliminating the asymmetry of information would deprive an individual of what is their essence, i.e. the taste of life. Having exactly the same state of knowledge for everyone would make everyday reality completely predictable and monotonous. However, F. A. von Hayek and M. Polanyi showed in their works that equality of knowledge is impossible – both fundamentally and physically. For more on this, see: Hayek (1996); Polanyi (1962).
6 They can be called public goods or whatever.
7 For more on this, see also: Block (1983, pp. 1–34).
8 For more on this topic see: Riesman (1994).
9 For more on the Austrian critique of the theory of public goods see: Wiśniewski (2018).
10 For more on this subject see: Armentano (2005).
11 In this paper, due to the limited content, only some (general) arguments will be presented against the claims suggesting the emergence of monopolies in unfettered markets. For more information see: Rothbard (2009, pp. 661–704).
12 As the theory of perfect competition presupposes. For more on its criticism from the perspective of the Austrian School, see: Kuropatwa (2010, pp. 31–46).
13 For more on this, see DiLorenzo, 1985, pp. 73–90.

References

Akerlof G., 1970, The market for lemons: qualitative uncertainty and the market mechanism, *Quarterly Journal of Economics*, 84, 488–500.
Armentano D., 2005, A critique of neoclassical and Austrian monopoly theory, https://mises.org/library/critique-neoclassical-and-austrian-monopoly-theory (accessed: 24. 08. 2018).
Arrow K. J., 1963, Uncertainty and the welfare economics of medical care', *The American Economic Review*, No. 5, pp. 941–973.
Berdine G., 2016, 'Uncertainty and the welfare economics of medical care: an Austrian rebuttal: Part 1', *The Southwest Respiratory and Critical Care Chronicles*, No. 16, pp. 57–61.
Berdine G., 2017a, 'Uncertainty and the welfare economics of medical care: an Austrian rebuttal: Part 2', *The Southwest Respiratory and Critical Care Chronicles*, No 17, pp. 63–67.

Berdine G., 2017b, 'Uncertainty and the welfare economics of medical care: an Austrian rebuttal-part 3', *The Southwest Respiratory and Critical Care Chronicles*, No. 19, pp. 25–29.

Block W., 1983, 'Public Goods and Externalities: The Case of Roads', *The Journal of Libertarian Studies*, No. 1, pp. 1–34.

DiLorenzo T., 1985, 'The Origins of Antitrust: An Interest-Group Perspective', *International Review of Law and Economics*, No. 1, pp. 73–90.

DiLorenzo T., 1996, 'The Myth of Natural Monopoly', *The Review of Austrian Economics*, No. 2, pp. 43–58.

DiLorenzo T., 2011, 'A note on the canard of 'asymmetric information' as a source of market failure', *Quarterly Journal of Austrian Economics*, No. 2, pp. 249–255.

Goodman J. C., Musgrave G. L., Herrick D. M., 2004, *Lives at risk. Single-payer national health insurance around the world*, USA: Rowman & Littlefield Publishers.

Hayek F. A., 1996, *Individualism and economic order*, USA: University of Chicago Press.

Holcombe R., 2007, A theory of the theory of public goods, *Review of Austrian Economics*, 1, 1–22.

Klein P. G., 2013, The Mises view: 'Healthcare and the free market', https://www.youtube.com/watch?v=8lOC2itCc6g (accessed: 10. 06. 2021).

Kuropatwa A., 2010, Problemy neoklasycznej teorii konkurencji [Problems of the neoclassical theory of competition], in M. Machaj (ed.), *Pod prąd głównego nurtu ekonomii* [Against the tide of mainstream economics], Warsaw: Instytut Ludwiga von Misesa, pp. 31–46.

Kwiatkowski S., 2010, Teoria dóbr publicznych i rynkowe mechanizmy ich produkcji [The theory of public goods and market mechanisms of their production], in M. Machaj (ed.), *Pod prąd głównego nurtu ekonomii* [Against the tide of mainstream economics], Warsaw: Instytut Ludwiga von Misesa, pp. 95–123.

Maxwell J. C., 2003, *There's no such thing as 'business' ethics: There's only one rule for making decisions*, USA: Warner Books.

Mises L., 1998, *Human action. A treatise on economics*, Auburn: Ludwig von Mises Institute.

Monkiewicz J., 2002, Prywatne ubezpieczenia zdrowotne w Unii Europejskiej [Private health insurance in the European Union], in J. Monkiewicz (ed.), *Ubezpieczenia w Unii Europejskiej* [Insurance in the European Union], Warsaw: Poltext.

Morris S., Devlin N., Parkin D., Spencer A., 2012, *Economic analysis in healthcare*, Great Britain: Wiley.

Polanyi M., 1962, *Personal knowledge: Towards a post-critical philosophy*, Chicago: University of Chicago Press.

Reed L. W., 2015, Rockefeller's standard oil company proved we needed antitrust laws to fight market monopolies, in L. W. Reed (ed.), *Excuse me, Professor: Challenging the myths of progressivism*, USA: Regnery Publishing, pp. 337–357.

Riesman G., 1994, *The real right to medical care versus socialized medicine*, USA: The Jefferson School of Philosophy, Economics & Psychology.

Rothbard M. N., 2009, *Man, economy, and state with power and market*, Auburn: Ludwig von Mises Institute.

Samuelson P. A., 1954, The pure theory of public expenditure, *Review of Economics and Statistics*, 4, 387–389.

Savedoff W. D., 2004, Kenneth Arrow and the birth of health economics, *Bulletin of the World Health Organization*, 2, 139–140.

Tannenhill L., Tannenhill M., 2009, *The market for liberty*, USA: Cobden Press/Fox & Wilkes/Laissez Faire Books.

Wiśniewski J. B., 2018, *The economics of law, order, and action: The logic of public goods*, London, New York: Routledge.

Part II

Universal (public) health system as an effect of state interventions

Introduction

The second part of the study deals with issues related to the functioning of universal (public) health systems and their characteristics. The analysis covered primarily issues related to the appropriate definition of such a system, the goals it is to pursue, the sources of its financing, and the concept and importance of health in the individual and social dimension.

This is to help better understand the principles of its functioning and the impact on the availability of medical services, health, or even the doctor–patient relationship. Thanks to this, it will also be possible to compare such a system more easily with market solutions characterized by a more diversified structure of financing access to medical services.

In order to better understand this issue, at the beginning, the theoretical aspects of interventionism are also analysed, starting from its definition and the type of individual interventions, and ending with their possible effects (consequences) for the market health system.

DOI: 10.4324/9781003258957-6

4 Interventionism in the health system

The definition and essence of interventionism

The issue of interventionism was gradually developed by successive representatives of the Austrian School from single interventions to a coherent general theory. The first economist to use the term in an economic sense was Mises (Huerta de Soto, 2009, p. 292). Successive interventions in the market economy over the years (including the health system) required appropriate analysis, which also influenced the development of the theory.[1] An important contribution in this regard must also be attributed to Rothbard, who, inter alia, made an appropriate classification of the various interventions.[2] For Rothbard (2009, p. 877), intervention is: 'the intrusion of aggressive physical force into society; it means the substitution of coercion for voluntary actions.'

This definition is very broad and has a praxeological character. From this perspective, it doesn't matter who intervenes: single bandit, mafia, or state. The fact that the economic analysis of interventionism concerns mainly state actions is because this institution has a monopoly on the use of force (or the threat of its use) in voluntary market relations. The institution of the state is not the subject of an ideological attack for the economist, but subject of study, as was the case with the market economy or socialism. Economics as a science strives to best understand the effects of actions taken in various economic systems, and this means that assumptions must be objective if it is to perform its function well.

As a rule, interventionism allows for the existence of a market economy in order to control its specific spheres. Interventionist measures used, for example, by political groups or key decision-makers in the country may take very different forms, which can ultimately be classified into three types of intervention: autistic, binary, and triangular. The first type of intervention means forcing the *intervener* [3] (e.g. the state) to force

DOI: 10.4324/9781003258957-7

an individual or a group of units to behave in a specific manner relating to that entity (group) or its assets at a time when no exchange is made with other market participants. Examples of such intervention include, for example, murder, ban on expression, or religious practices. Importantly, this type of intervention does not lead to a forced transfer of goods or services to the entity making the intervention. The second type, binary intervention, consists in forcing such a transfer. The individual must surrender some of their goods or services, under threat of force by the *intervener*. Examples of this type of intervention include, for example, taxes, conscription, and slavery. On the other hand, a triangular intervention takes place when the intervener forces an exchange (or prohibits it) between two parties to the transaction but does not itself participate in it – it boils down to the role of a kind of intermediary influencing the terms of the exchange. Examples include price control (e.g. setting a maximum or minimum price) or licensing a profession. A common feature of these interventions is the existence of a hegemonic relationship between the *intervener* and the individuals they concern. The intervening entity always benefits at the expense of individuals, only in the third case it is possible to benefit from one of the parties to the transaction, e.g. as a result of restriction of competition by state regulations – then the harm will be suffered by consumers and entities willing to enter a given market (Rothbard, 2009, pp. 877–878).

Economics does not presuppose the existence, activity, or function of a state that is excluded from these considerations. Therefore, the legitimacy of certain actions taken by the state should also result from economic premises. As Mises (1998a, p. 718) put it:

> The problem of interventionism is not a problem of the correct delimitation of the 'natural,' 'just,' and 'adequate' tasks of state and government. The issue is: How does a system of interventionism work? Can it realize those ends which people, in resorting to it, want to?

This applies to every aspect of state activity: road construction, national defence, pension systems, and healthcare. From the economic point of view, it is unacceptable to say that a given activity of the state in the economy should be excluded from economic analysis, as it is generally not recognized as the domain of the market and market (and economic) laws do not apply here.

Individual interventions are measures taken to achieve the intended goals. However, these measures or plans for their use may (and usually are) very different from each other. While the goal remains basically the same, the desire to improve the welfare of a society or a country, the variants of its implementation remain quite different. The basis for the political struggle between particular groups is precisely the manner and scope of the use of interventionist measures. In fact, each grouping has more or less different plans, which is the basis for the political struggle and the object of soliciting votes. Mises (1998a, p. 727) described the problem as follows:

> All this passionate praise of the supereminence of government action is but a poor disguise for the individual interventionist's self-deification. The great god State is a great god only because it is expected to do exclusively what the individual advocate of interventionism wants to see achieved. Only that plan is genuine which the individual planner fully approves. All other plans are simply counterfeit.

It can therefore be concluded that individual interventionists do not support interventionism at all, but their specific plans. They can unite for a common goal when, for example, a part of society begins to consciously and increasingly actively undermine the sense of making any interventions in the market economy. However, there are also cases where it is quite easy to discern some internal contradiction in the actions or plans of interventionists. An example should be social/health insurance. If a certain political grouping today demands, for example, extending the scope of public health insurance or lowering the retirement age, pointing to the fact that it is the domain of the state and a human right, such postulates constitute a hidden criticism of its initial activities in this area. In the late nineteenth and early twentieth centuries, when the first public social security programmes were established, they did not contain any extensive coverage. These programmes were very modest and today, if another group wanted to limit the modern, extended ranges to their original size, it would certainly be criticized by their political rivals (and perhaps part of society as well). Nor can it be argued that the previous solutions were adapted to the social needs of the time. For example, in the Bismarck system, retirement privileges began to be granted from the age of 70, while the average life expectancy was about 40 years, and the minimum contribution period was 30 years (Pieńkowska-Kamieniecka & Rutecka, 2014, p. 20). Also, healthcare only guaranteed access to specific medical services in the event of loss of capacity for work due to an accident or disease.[4] It is a paradox that initial social security systems or programmes would be unacceptable today. The reason they are not criticized is that the modest momentum in their introduction allowed the achievement of certain political goals at relatively low cost. However, this did not prevent them from growing to an exorbitant size over the course of many decades.

If the direction to a more extensive range of such programmes (and interventionism) is considered to be the subject of economic analysis, then the opposite direction should also be – from interventionism to a pure market economy.[5] There are many different examples of interventions. Each of them requires appropriate analysis and often brings different results.

One of the more famous examples is the milk price control case described by Mises.[6] In a given economy, there is a milk market that is not subject to intervention. However, the government believes that the price of milk is too high, so that part of the population, especially children, cannot consume enough of it. In order to improve the situation, the government introduces a maximum price (below the market price). The government is counting on the fact that by artificially lowering the price, more people will be able to afford milk. However, the effects of this intervention are quite different from those assumed. The milk market consists of many enterprises (milk producers) who try to meet the needs of their customers in the best possible way. So, they employ primary and secondary factors of production and, as a result, incur costs. The amount of these costs is not the same for everyone. The most efficient producers achieve the highest profits, others lower profits, and the rest of them lose and, as a result, they fall out of the market. However, artificially lowering the market price, the part of the producers who have the highest costs but remain in the market will not be able to cover all costs from falling (artificially) revenues and will eventually fall out of the market. In addition, some of the more efficient producers may switch to the production of more profitable goods, such as butter or cream – there is no price control in these markets, so the achievable profits may be higher than in the milk market. Ultimately, the supply of milk on the market decreases and the number of people willing to buy it at a certain price increases. The price, although lowered thanks to the government, did not contribute to the increase in milk consumption. The government, of course, sees this problem. The situation after the intervention is less desirable than that before the intervention. The government may admit its mistake and withdraw from its plans – then the situation will return to normal relatively quickly. However, if the government continues to achieve its goal, it will have to introduce further interventions. This may be, for example, the introduction of maximum prices among suppliers of milk producers, e.g. feed producers, and then among suppliers of feed producers, etc., up to the owners of the primary factors of production. In addition, the government will have to introduce similar regulations in other markets, otherwise the capital will go to less regulated related markets or, for example, to luxury goods markets. This example shows that the initial, single intervention gives rise to another, and as a result, the government begins to control other parts of the economy, even though it had not planned it before. Of course, the government can backtrack on its decisions, but it usually doesn't. This may be due to a reluctance to admit a mistake, the belief that political competitors will point out the government's mistakes and want to introduce their own, more interventionist programmes, or blame a deteriorating market economy (e.g. producers). For economic analysis, the reasons why governments decide to intervene again are irrelevant. What matters is the very fact of making them and their effects.

The process of making subsequent interventions can be very long, but it will not last forever. Eventually, the government will be forced to control the entire economy. The price system, and hence the profit and loss mechanism, will not fulfil its useful function in the appropriate allocation of capital and in satisfying the needs of consumers. The government will have to properly instruct producers what to produce and in what quantities and to whom to sell. Naturally, the purpose of the example above is not to prove that intervention in the milk market leads to socialism. It is led by the consistently applied interventionism, or in other words, the system of the (increasingly) hampered market economy. Mises's important contribution to the development of the theory of interventionism was precisely the demonstration of the dynamic nature of interventionism. The maintenance by governments of isolated and non-widening interventions in the market economy is not possible due to different effects than assumed, which is a kind of moral hazard for governments in the form of a desire to improve the situation. As Mises (1998b, pp. 77, 91) stated:

> Interventionism is not an economic system, that is, it is not a method which enables people to achieve their aims. It is merely a system of procedures which disturb and eventually destroy the market economy. It hampers production and impairs satisfaction of needs. It does not make people richer; it makes people poorer. [...]
>
> Interventionist measures lead to conditions which, from the standpoint of those who recommend them, are actually less desirable than those they are designed to alleviate. They create unemployment, depression, monopoly, distress.

The analysis of the effects of interventionism is not easy due to, inter alia, constantly changing and complex market conditions and the emergence of subsequent interventions that have a direct or indirect impact on these conditions. Following Rothbard, however, it can be said that free exchange leads to the maximization of social utility understood as all utilities achieved by individuals on the market. Under market conditions, both parties to the transaction, by definition (ex-ante) benefit from the exchange, otherwise it would not take place. Intervention, on the other hand, consists in forcing people to take actions that they would not have taken otherwise. Therefore, interventionism always leads to a decline in the utility of the individuals it covers. On the other hand, the entity making the intervention and, possibly, in the case of a triangular intervention, one of the parties to the transaction gains. Since utility is subjective and cannot be represented in numbers, the state cannot prove that social utility increases. For example, it is not possible to prove that taxes imposed on the rich cause less loss of utility in them, and greater loss in people with relatively lower income or wealth. Of course, people make mistakes and it may turn out that after the transaction (ex post) their usefulness has decreased or has not increased as much as expected. However, in a free market, people can take measures to avoid a similar situation in the future. And in the case of subsequent interventions, the individual has very limited possibilities to counteract them (Rothbard, 2009, pp. 878–891).

Another important feature of interventionism is also worth mentioning. Very often, interventions that appear at first sight to control producers are in fact intended to influence consumers indirectly. For example, if the state wants to reduce the consumption of carbonated sweet drinks and increase water or juice, it may impose additional taxes on the sale of this product, introduce regulations limiting its supply, or subsidize producers of healthy drinks. The fact that a given intervention does not directly concern the consumer may be caused by the fear of a decrease in support or the awareness of the lower effectiveness of such intervention. Moreover, they perceive the effects of interventions involving consumers much more easily than interventions involving producers. Due to the large number of interventions and the complexity of market processes, it is usually difficult for consumers to see cause-and-effect relationships. Also, favouring lobbying producers at the expense of competition (e.g. through a licensing system, capital requirements, safety standards, etc.) is an indirect influence on the decisions of consumers, for whom the costs of lost opportunities in such a situation are not noticeable.

Selected possible interventions on the healthcare market and their effects

The dynamic nature of interventionism can also be demonstrated in the market health system. The proliferation of interventions does not lead to the establishment of socialism in the health system,[7] but to increasing state control of markets that provide society with the medical (health) goods and services it needs. The scope of such interventions can vary greatly, from single interventions to integrated, predetermined health plans designed to provide comprehensive and (mostly) free access to these goods and services. The dynamics of interventionist processes can therefore be considered both from the stages of individual interventions leading ultimately to public healthcare (a single payer system) or from such a system, if it has already been fully implemented, to subsequent actions of the state aimed at maintaining its functioning. Subsequent interventions, as mentioned earlier, do not prove the success of previous interventions, but their failure.

Due to the large variety of universal (public) health systems in individual countries, the case of each of them should be subject to a thorough cause-and-effect analysis. For example, the United States of America does not have a single payer system like European countries or Canada. The history of successive interventions in the US health system shows, however, that they create an increasingly integrated (although not planned top-down) structure limiting market processes and directing the US health system to the state-funded single payer system. An important task of economics is to demonstrate the effects that subsequent interventions bring or may bring.

The introduction of a more or less extensive universal (public) healthcare system has very serious socio-economic consequences. One of the most serious is the disturbance of the relationship between direct and indirect (through third-party payers) purchasing of medical goods and services by consumers. The state, instead of the consumer, makes a lot of decisions, including: what goods and services are to be included in the scope of such a system, whether and what the level of payment is to be, what are the standards for approving drugs, technologies, or particular medical professions for use, or medical facilities providing the services (under the general system) are to be public or private, etc. The effects of these interventions are primarily such that the consumer who does not pay the bills out of their own pocket has a problem with real cost estimation. It is not able to accurately assess whether a given good or service is easily or difficult to access. On the market, they could, for example, insure themself against certain events, and pay the rest out of their own pocket with competing suppliers. However, they would be aware of the consequences of their choices. In addition, any norms or standards for approving drugs or technologies on the market replace the subjective opinion of the consumer regarding their suitability. Also, regulations on medical professions (e.g. through a system of non-market licences) limit the consumer's choice and knowledge of alternative treatments. The activities of producers and suppliers are then aimed at meeting these top-down requirements, which also generates higher costs and extends the time of introducing new goods and services to use. The development of innovative solutions is either eliminated or limited. Producers no longer estimate the potential demand reported by consumers based on their value judgements (or at least to a limited extent) but try to predict what action the state (given government) will take. Disrupting the processes of consumer evaluation by subsequent interventions negatively affects the satisfaction of their needs and contributes to the problems of economic calculation – arising when the state tries to take over the role of the market. However, the price structure in the market for final and capital goods and services was originally subordinated to the consumer's sovereignty. In a market economy, each participant is both a consumer and a producer. On the one hand, everyone sets their own requirements for the goods and services they are willing to buy and, on the other hand, as an employee or entrepreneur, they try to meet them towards other consumers. As Mises (2012, p. 20) put it:

> Now, in the economic system of private ownership of the means of production, the system of computation by value is necessarily employed by each independent member of society. Everybody participates in its emergence in a double way: on the one hand as a consumer and on the other as a producer. As a consumer he establishes a scale of valuation for goods ready for use in consumption. As a producer he puts goods of a higher order into such use as produces the greatest return. In this way all goods of a higher order receive a position in the scale of valuations in accordance with the immediate state of social conditions of production and of social needs. Through the interplay of these two processes of valuation, means will be afforded for governing both consumption and production by the economic principle throughout. Every graded system of pricing proceeds from the fact that men always and ever harmonized their own requirements with their estimation of economic facts.

The artificially stimulated demand for medical services leads to social pressure to spend more and more money on their delivery. The state therefore raises taxes (or premiums) on the basis of the right to healthcare. However, it is not possible to constantly raise taxes or incur debts for these purposes. First, the non-net beneficiary part of society begins to express its dissatisfaction with the ever-increasing levies.[8] Secondly, the state has other competing goals that also require resources (taxes), e.g. road construction, pension insurance, national defence, etc. Third, if the consumer spends only a fraction of their cost on certain goods and services, they will not abstain from consumption. At the same time, the illusion of free healthcare creates the illusion of its abundance. However, when the almost unlimited right to healthcare of one citizen meets the same law, successive citizens begin to compete with each other for, as it turns out, rare goods and medical services. In response to these actions, the state introduces various forms of rationing, which may further accelerate the use of (still) available resources.

So it is a version of the so-called tragedy of the commons, a case described by Hardin (1968, pp. 1243–1248), where dairy farmers, in order to increase their profits, over-exploited the common resources (pastures), not caring for the interests of other farmers and ultimately leading to the degradation of pastures. The solution to this problem was to separate private property through a fencing system, so that each farmer had an interest in the proper exploitation of their pastures.[9] Thus, private property introduces order to social relations and enables rational decisions based on economic calculation. Often, in order to deal with similar problems, the necessary state intervention, e.g. in the form of issuing appropriate regulations or imposing taxes, is also indicated. However, considering the use of such measures in relation to universal (public) health systems, it should be said that it is such interventions that are the main cause of problems (tragedies), not the solutions to them. If the state creates its insurance programme for all members of society, then, unlike real insurance, taxes and regulations abolish the limits of using a common healthcare resource. Under market conditions, insurers create specific risk groups consisting of members with similar probability of using medical services. The premium paid (net) reflects the insurance risk. Therefore, these are the boundaries that insurers set for individual members of risk groups, ensuring their relative homogeneity, which is a condition for effective assistance to their members when the need arises.

Also, local communities can create various quasi-insurance programmes. In the past, for example, fraternal associations were very popular. These institutions brought together city residents or people working in a given profession and provided them with access to various benefits, such as payment of funds as a result of an accident or the death of a member.[10] Their advantage was, among other things, that local communities have an interest in supporting each other and at the same time making sure that no one tries to excessively use the benefits they are entitled to. Joining a new, anonymous member was associated with their acceptance of the prevailing rules. To simplify it, it can be said that the principles of operation of such associations were similar to those of modern mutual insurance companies.

Meanwhile, public insurance makes the restrictions created by insurance companies or other associations disappear, while at the same time extending the scope of anonymity of such programmes, which creates the illusion of a real possibility for unhampered use of medical services. A resident from the east of Poland will not wonder if their frequent use of such insurance does not limit funds for a resident of the western part of Poland. They will focus on satisfying their needs in the best and fastest way (at an artificially low price), which is evidence of a kind of competition in general (public) health systems and a result of state interventionism.

If the price of a given goods and services has been artificially lowered or is unrelated to the rational pricing of risk, there is pressure to increase them. Due to the fact that patients cannot pay the doctor directly from their own pocket, they try to do it through other forms of payment or, in other words, bribes in exchange for preferential treatment. From an economic point of view, a bribe testifies to the failure of public institutions to provide needed medical goods and services. The fact that a person received the medical services they needed thanks to a bribe at the expense of another person does not change the fact that the supply-demand relations have been disturbed. Even if such a situation did not take place, someone would not ultimately gain access to medical services. In the marketplace, this problem is solved by rising prices and profits, which encourages suppliers (and competitors) to increase supply and reduce costs

Producers also treat this type of payment as an effective means to achieve the goals. Instead of being subject to the laws of the market, they start to take a defensive stance. In order to maintain the current market position, they undertake numerous lobbying activities aimed at limiting competition, often under the pretext of providing high-quality services in order to care for the health of patients. This is one of the reasons why the medical industry has so many licences, quality standards, product control, and other regulations that are a substitute for consumer sovereignty and competition processes.

Part of society, dissatisfied with the functioning of the universal (public) healthcare system, reaches for market alternatives: direct payments, health insurance, medical subscriptions, or, as a last resort, charity aid. In this way, you pay double for the goods and services in question, in a sense subsidizing defective public systems and, in part, camouflaging their problems with ensuring adequate availability of medical goods and services. However, the number of people willing to purchase private alternatives is relatively smaller. Additionally, government regulations hinder the functioning of these market processes, increasing manufacturers' costs and limiting competition and innovation. Therefore, the prices of certain goods and services are relatively higher than they would be in the case of unhampered market processes. Interestingly, politicians are often among the first buyers of market alternatives. A good example here is Sweden, where politicians were among the first beneficiaries of having private health insurance as an alternative to the many months of waiting for, among others, specialist services such as surgery (Bylund, 2014).

The society uses market alternatives and is aware of the problems of public systems, but at the same time has a problem with recognizing that market solutions are not only an addition or supplement to public systems, but a condition for the efficient provision of the necessary medical goods and services to society. Interventionism in the healthcare system leads to the consolidation or even deepening of the asymmetry of information. The consumer does not make decisions on their own behalf, choosing among competing suppliers and advisers. All decisions about what is to be produced and which entities are to approve e.g. drugs or technologies are made without their participation. Moreover, rising costs and concerns about the spectre of expenses exceeding the financial capacity of a single person, to some extent, consolidate the belief in society that a universal (public) healthcare system is necessary – despite its shortcomings. This leads to successive interventions, this time to remedy the unintended effects of previous market economy interventions.

Notes

1 For more on the development of Mises's theory of interventionism, see: Lavoie (1982, pp. 169–183).
2 Some differences can be found between the definitions of interventionism in Mises and Rothbard, but they are not significant for the issues discussed in this book.
3 Other names Rothbard uses are *invader* or *aggressor*.

4 Fr. von Bismarck, de facto, pursued political goals by successfully adapting the postulates of his political opponents as his own, thus depriving them of some of their arguments in the struggle for power. The various social security programmes were thus introduced, at least in part, for political reasons.

5 If an interventionist criticizes the analysis of a pure market economy as an impossible or even imaginary state, then at the same time they should have the same position towards the other extreme system, i.e. socialism. For various reasons, however, this is often not the case, because de facto socialism also uses force against, or threatens to use, individuals.

6 Interestingly, this is not only a good academic example with little economic impact. In fact, during World War II, many countries used product price controls in response to inflation induced to finance the increasing war spending. It is also interesting to note that in the US price controls have led to a non-market increase in health insurance demand, which is an interesting example of the 'interface' of economic theory (in Mises's example) with economic reality and this work.

7 This term refers to the economy as a whole in which there is no private ownership of the means of production.

8 It may also lead to a slowdown in the growth rate of expenses.

9 It is also worth mentioning that other solutions to this problem have been described by E. Ostrom. For more on this subject see: Ostrom (1990).

10 Northern Italy in the late nineteenth and early twentieth centuries can be indicated as an effective historical example of this type of initiative. For more on this subject see: Tedeschi (2015, pp. 47–64).

References

Bylund P., 2014, The market is taking over Sweden's health care, https://mises.org/library/market-taking-over-sweden´s-health-care (accessed: 28. 08. 2018).

Hardin G., 1968, The tragedy of the commons, *Science*, 3859, 1243–1248.

Huerta De Soto J., 2009, *The theory of dynamic efficiency*, USA, Canada: Routledge.

Lavoie D. C., 1982, The development of the Misesian theory of interventionism, in I. Kirzner (ed.), *Method, process and the Austrian Economics essays in honor of Ludwig von Mises*, Lexington Books, Lexington: DC Heath and Company, pp. 169–183.

Mises L., 1998a, *Human action. A treatise on economics*, Auburn: Ludwig von Mises Institute.

Mises L., 1998b, *Interventionism: An economic analysis*, New York: The Foundation for Economic Education.

Mises L., 2012, *Economic calculation in the socialist commonwealth*, Auburn: Ludwig von Mises Institute.

Ostrom E., 1990, *Governing the commons: The evolution of institutions for collective action*, Cambridge: Cambridge University Press.

Pieńkowska-Kamieniecka S., Rutecka J., 2014, System emerytalny w Niemczech – analiza aktualnych tendencji na tle dotychczasowego procesu reformowania [Pension system in Germany – analysis of current trends against the background of the reform process to date'], *Ubezpieczenia społeczne. Teoria i praktyka*, 6, 19–33.

Rothbard M. N., 2009, *Man, economy, and state with power and market*, Auburn: Ludwig von Mises Institute.

Tedeschi P., 2015, A new welfare system: Friendly societies in Eastern Lombardy from 1860 to 1914, in B. Harris (ed.), *Welfare and old age in Europe and North America: The development of social insurance*, London, New York: Routledge, pp. 47–64.

5 Universal (public) health system

Definition of the universal (public) health system

The universal (public) health system is not the result of independent consumer decisions, but the result of a regulatory framework defined by the state. Perhaps this openness of public institutions indirectly speaks in favour of interventionism. The perspective of the state's responsibility for the fate of an individual, to some extent, frees them from decision-making and responsibility in the area of their own health by creating a system to ensure their safety. The goals of the universal and market-based health system remain the same – to provide the society with necessary medical (health) goods and services. The question that economics is trying to answer boils down to the legitimacy of the measures that are to serve this purpose and the effects of their application.

One of the features of interventionism is that it is quite difficult to identify examples of identical interventions applied across countries in the field of public health systems (or universal health systems). While the very definition of an intervention is quite broad, there are many examples of it. The same is true of the concept of healthcare in the literature on the subject defined as: 'Goods and services used as inputs to produce health. Some analyses consider people's own time and knowledge used to maintain and promote health, in addition to conventional health care inputs' (Folland et al., 2012, p. 551).

However, as mentioned earlier, basically each of the beneficiaries imagines these outlays differently. Of course, this image is about their needs, not the rest of society. Healthcare is not one-size-fits-all. These are a variety of medical goods and services that everyone needs depending on their needs. An elderly and chronically ill person needs a different set of goods and services than a young and healthy person. Moreover, each entity or person making the intervention has its own

DOI: 10.4324/9781003258957-8

plan for their implementation. Therefore, individual public health systems, more or less, differ from one another. However, the question may be asked whether the state cannot finance access to healthcare only to those most in need of it. Why, as world prosperity increases and economic development continues, is there no minimum public health system for the poorest? When trying to answer this question, one should take into account the economic consequences of this state of affairs. The question of the functioning of such a minimal system is not limited only to itself, but de facto, it also concerns the entire economy. It can be concluded that then two health systems would function: minimal (state-owned) and comprehensive (complementary, market-based) – covering the rest of the society. It should be noted, however, that in such an arrangement the state does not undertake only and exclusively to refrain from intervening in the market healthcare system, but also in other parts of the economy.[1]

If it is recognized that only a small part of society cannot or does not have sufficient resources to take care of itself, the rest of society can do it. In order for the majority of society to take appropriate action to this end, it must have certain resources at its disposal. Markets, too, must therefore be subordinated to their decisions. The state, wishing to introduce, for example, new taxes in order to implement an ambitious investment programme limits the amount of funds at the disposal of an individual. It is not possible to conduct an experiment whether a given entity wants to allocate its resources to health insurance or, for example, to purchase a computer, and to tax it or not. Even if its decisions do not concern the purchase of medical goods and services, in the name of respect for its freedom and responsibility for its own decisions, it cannot be prohibited from doing so. Such a society will therefore not be willing to accept new taxes. Hence the conclusion that the market health system is an element of the market economy and any state interference, also in its other areas, has an indirect impact on this system. The existence and proper functioning of the market health system depends not only on the lack of state intervention in itself, but also (indirectly) in other parts of the economy.

It can also be stated, with some simplification, that the universal health system is to some extent complementary with other state interventions in the economy. The universality of this system results, inter alia, from the fact that by embracing every member of society, it gives the state the means both to create a universal health protection system and, indirectly, it can serve as a justification for other interventions in the economy. It is not only a theoretical case. Often times, the public fails to see that a state's withdrawal from one area of intervention does not have to be sufficient. Due to the disturbed supply-demand relations, it is currently difficult to state what expenditures on healthcare are needed. In which segments are they too high and in which too low? Of course, unhampered market processes in the health system can bring very positive results also if the state does not withdraw from its interventions from other parts of the economy. However, the purpose of this argument is to draw attention to the fact that individual parts of the economy cannot be treated as isolated islands. Therefore, instead of talking about the public healthcare system (and its economy), it is more reasonable, from the economic perspective, to use the term universal (public) health system, which can be defined as:

> Systematic use by the state of interventions (binary and triangular), involving consumers and producers of medical (health) goods and services, aimed at forcing them to make decisions that would not be made by these entities in the consumption and production of these goods and services, if the interventions did not take place.[2]

The economic aspect of the above definition draws attention to the existence of opportunity costs for interventionism. Therefore, one cannot focus solely on the analysis of interventionism in the healthcare system without any reflection on the effects on the rest of the economy or society.[3] As Hazlitt (2008, p. 5) stated: 'The art of economics consists in looking not merely at the immediate hut at the longer effects of any act or policy; it consists in tracing the consequences of that policy not merely for one group but for all groups.'[4]

Interventionists may, however, argue that failure by the state to intervene can have dire consequences due to market failures. The problem of asymmetric information is particularly often pointed to as its alleged failure in the market healthcare system. Criticism of individual cases of market failure has already been presented in Part I. However, in the context of the problem of asymmetric information, it is worth paying attention to the internal contradiction of the arguments cited. According to them, state intervention in the market health system is necessary due to the fact that producers (sellers) have more knowledge about their products and thus they will be able to deceive unaware consumers. Without specialist knowledge, a consumer will never be sure whether a given good or medical service will improve or maintain their health. Therefore, state intervention is necessary to effectively protect society against dishonest producers (sellers). However, if the consumer does not have sufficient knowledge to determine from which manufacturers they should purchase the given medical goods or services, they will also not be able to determine whether experts hired by the state are acting in their favour or not. It will not be able to say whether the solutions (interventions) of party X are better than those of party Y. The information gap will still exist. Society will not be able to assess the justification and effects of the intervention. Therefore, it should be considered a paradox that politicians consider citizens competent to elect them during elections, at the same time stating that they are not competent enough to freely decide about the purchase of the medical goods and services they need. In other words, citizens are guided by wisdom and insight and caution in their elections, qualities that unexpectedly disappear after the elections are completed.

The above argumentation can also be extended by asking the question why the problem of asymmetric information should concern only the producer–consumer relationship. In the market conditions, in principle, every producer of final goods and services has its suppliers who also have their suppliers, etc. There are markets for factors of production. There is no single large enterprise that directly manages all stages of production within a large organizational structure. Each company has a specific specialization that is constantly deepening. Therefore, accepting the theory of information asymmetry, one should agree that it also occurs in the producer X (seller) – producer Y (buyer) relationship. The markets for the factors of production would then have to undergo constant collapses, as a last resort, preventing the emergence of final goods and services of adequate quality. Producers of lower-order goods would be at the mercy of producers of higher-order goods. Reducing the above claims to their logical consequences would mean that the state must also deal with strict control of the factor markets.[5] The state would have to decide for entrepreneurs what products are to be purchased, in what quantities and at what *prices*. The image of such an economic system is nothing but socialism.

Of course, there are no such collapses (crises) in the factor markets. This is because unhampered market processes do not lead to the creation, but to the removal of asymmetric information, which is one of the conditions for satisfying consumer needs adequately.

It can also be concluded that the problem of asymmetric information (or uncertainty) may also be exacerbated by announcements and reforms of public health systems. In fact, no one, apart from the initiators of these reforms, is able to find out in the maze of regulatory changes, let alone their exact impact on access to specific medical services.

General principles of operation and goals

The general principles on which universal health systems have been based have remained the same since their inception – the use of systematic interventions. Only the means by which one tries to achieve the set goals can change. The means for their implementation are individual interventions, which, according to Folland et al. (2012, p. 398) are manifested in three activities (groups): 'provision of goods and services, redistribution, and regulation. Governments have pursued each of these activities in the health economy.'

On the other hand, the basic, general purpose of the existence of such a system can be defined as an attempt to systematically provide the society with the necessary medical (health) goods and services, the purchase of which under market conditions (in the opinion of the governing bodies) would not be possible in the scale of the entire society. There are causal relationships between the three above-mentioned interventions. In order to provide the society with medical goods and services, the state must first produce them or purchase them from private suppliers, first specifying the requirements (for consumers) that they must meet. In order for these activities to be possible, the state must have adequate funds from private sources – without them it will not be possible to maintain appropriate institutions and redistribute funds between individual members of society. For this purpose, appropriate legal acts (subsequent regulations) are created, imposing the obligation to transfer some private funds (income) to previously set purposes, e.g. in the form of taxes or contributions (premiums).

Due to the fact that the universal health system is non-market, the methods of assessing its results also differ from the market ones. On the market, it is easy to assess the degree of meeting consumer needs, e. g. on the basis of the profit and loss account or taking into account rankings of institutions or people working in a given profession, created on the basis of opinions expressed by consumers. Meanwhile, in the case of the universal health system, other criteria are used – inter alia, due to its compulsory nature. Frequent examples are the size of public expenditures allocated to healthcare (e.g. in relation to GDP or the state budget) or the number of insured persons. However, these criteria are not at all synonymous with getting better results. Very often, in order to improve the functioning of such systems, it is recommended to increase the expenditure. However, it is a mistake to equate an increase in financial resources with an increase in the supply of necessary medical goods and services – and these are often missing due to the disturbance of market relations. Medicines, medica equipment, or doctors are not idly waiting for patients in warehouses and offices due to lack of funds. The amount of drugs, medical equipment, or doctors is insufficient due to artificially stimulated demand or artificially limited supply. Therefore, increasing outlays only exacerbates the shortcomings of public systems without contributing to the improvement of their performance, much to the disappointment and confusion of the public. It is also a good example of where means are confused with ends, leading to further interventions and even greater statism. Moreover, even if increased inputs improve results, this does not at all prove the need for public systems. In this case, economics draws attention to the ratio of inputs to outputs, which is rare in political debates where participants focus especially on the first variable.

In the market conditions, the producer who suffers losses (which does not adequately meet the needs of consumers) falls out of the market and is replaced by more enterprising competitors. However, in the case of the universal health system, there is no such alternative. It is only possible to replace the plan of one party with the plan of party y, but the principles under which this system operates remain the same. It also often happens that the issues of improving the functioning of such systems are a hot topic of pre-election discussions, and no actions are taken after their completion. This is so, inter alia, because any changes could be associated with a decrease in the support of a part of the society[6] for the government planning such changes.

In some countries (e.g. Switzerland or the Netherlands) it was decided to involve private entities more. However, it should be emphasized that it was the implementation not so much of market solutions as private entities into the framework of public systems. Private entities supplying society with medical goods and services do so based on top-down guidelines, not market laws. They are not market systems as they are sometimes referred to. Further systematic interventions are made in them. The benefits offered by private institutions may be related to e.g. better resource management or management which results in lower costs, but they are still subject to many regulations.[7] Interestingly, the introduction of such solutions[8] was intended more to maintain public systems than to transform them into a market alternative. A good example is the reform of the Dutch healthcare system in 2006. As Gorajek (2013, p. 305) points out:

> The Minister of Health of the Kingdom of the Netherlands, speaking about the goals of the health reform introduced in 2006, did not focus on such items as putting the patient at the center of the system or improving satisfaction with the perception of the

health system, as we often hear in discussions of our politicians. The Dutch reform was introduced in order to: 'create a chance to maintain universal access to medical services at a level not significantly different from the scope before the reform'. In short, its aim was to maintain the status quo and prevent the deterioration of access or exclusion of a large group of citizens from the health care system.

The side effect of these processes is therefore a permanent monopoly (or quasi-monopoly) as the state continues to claim the right to take action to improve the situation despite previous failures. Such systems are not well prepared for the major demographic changes that are already taking place in societies. There is often talk of new challenges or goals for public systems, but these are merely nice-sounding semantic statements. The state, for its part, can only propose further interventions.

Sources of funding

To implement their objectives, specific public institutions must have adequate funds from private sources. To this end, the state must also determine on what terms the redistribution of funds between specific members of the public is to take place. The transfer of funds is also one of the basic differences between individual public systems. Already the first two public systems differed in this respect. In the British system, the source of financing the universal health system was taxes while the German system used premiums. The third option is a combination of the two. However, from the economic perspective, the form of taxation is secondary. What matters the most is the amount of taxation. What matters for an individual is the amount of funds they will be deprived of and what they can receive for it instead. Whether for example 2,400 USD per year is being taken from Smith in the form of a tax or contribution has less (or even none) meaning for him than the amount of the tax. Hence if Smith disagrees with such a state of affairs, he will be dissatisfied not so much with the form of taxation as with its amount.

Some may argue, however, that there is a difference. For example, a tax relief can be obtained from the collected premium; thanks to that Smith will be able to maintain some money, and that is not possible in the case of a tax. In fact, this is the confirmation of the above argument. A tax credit may cause that even the taxpayer is still charged 2,400 USD per year for healthcare, it reduces taxes paid by them (e.g. by 1,200 USD per year).[9] What is extremely important, Smith (or speaking more in general, society) will keep these 1,200 USD annually only when the state will not compensate for this reduced tax revenue and introduce new taxes or incur new debts. Thus, the tax credit system makes sense only then, if it reduces the total public expenditure and do not cause new budget deficits. In this situation, the state will have less funds for the implementation of its other purposes and if it does not give up on some of them, new taxes will be created to compensate for the tax credit. So, Smith will lose in the new taxes everything that he saved due to tax credit. In this situation, the redistribution of income will be made no longer only by the premium, but also through new imposition. Its reach will expand. New imposition, although directly not related to healthcare, in an economic sense, will serve to further fund it at a specified level. The state is not usually interested in reducing the total level of expenditure, i.e., it agrees on tax credits, but at the same time introduces new impositions so that the previous level of total expenditure can be maintained. This also leads to a dangerous situation in which it seems that the costs of healthcare incurred by individual members of society are falling (thanks to the tax credit and payers of the third party), which may result in even greater demand combined with constantly growing general level of healthcare expenditure. This is because the new impositions are spread over the entire society and beneficiaries of health systems may not even perceive their growth. For when society bears only a fraction of costs or expenses it does not pay sufficient attention to their constant growth.

Employer's participation (obligatory or voluntary) in financing employee's access to healthcare is confusing as well. And it does not matter whether the healthcare is public or private. Because in the economic sense, employees (not the employer) finance this access (e.g., through insurance). When hiring a new employee an employer is guided by economic calculation. They expect that additional (extreme) revenues related to this employment will be higher than additional (extreme) costs; otherwise, the employment of an additional employee would not make sense. If the state imposes an obligation on the employer to finance health insurance for the employee (e.g., in the amount of 50% of the premium), this does not lead to a nominal growth of the employee's salary, in the amount of this share, but it reduces the employee's net income instead. The employer's financial contribution is visible only from the point of view of the regulations (i. e., on paper). The employer may increase the nominal remuneration of the employee only if they reduce other costs — for example other employees' remuneration or costs of other factors of production. Also, in the case of group private health insurance constituting the so-called expansion employee benefits, the employer bears their costs from sources that could be spent on higher remuneration (or other objectives). The fact that this is not happening often results from the fact that employees' private group health insurance, through a workplace, gives much better insurance conditions than they could get as individual clients. For employees, for example, 100 USD per month for such insurance gives greater benefits than the increase in net pay by the amount mentioned. For the employer, in turn, offering such programmes constitutes an additional form of competition for employees, affects better working conditions, and therefore produces a good image for the company.

Increasing expenditures for the universal health system may also take place without the growth of taxes or increasing the deficit. In this situation, the state would have to limit expenditures for other purposes. Various goals that the state tries to achieve are therefore, in a certain sense, competitive. For example, resignation from one goal comes at the expense of the other one and resisting one social group brings support from the other one. The state is constantly facing the dilemma of achieving specific objectives at the expense of others. Should funds be allocated to improve road infrastructure or healthcare? If the state considers that the expenditure should be increased for healthcare, it must determine specifically which objectives will be funded: on the increases to pay doctors and nurses or maybe for the construction of new medical facilities? However, even in the case of assigning funds for relevant purposes, public institutions that do not have access to a profit and loss account will not be able to correctly specify whether the expenditure is sufficient or not. Without the freedom of consumers' choice and their value judgements, it will not be possible to check if the amount of tax or premium is too high, too low, or adequate. In the first two cases, this leads to increasing discomfort (reduction of utility) of individuals.

In fact, budgets that have public institutions financing access to specific health goods and services should not be considered as reliable because they are not the result of market economic calculation. Under the market conditions, economic calculation is possible due to the existence of the prices of final goods and prices factors of production. On this basis, you can easily determine profits or losses and take appropriate action in the future. Although prices expressed in money do not replace the valuation of consumers, they do constitute an easy tool for entrepreneurs, through which, on the basis of profit and loss account, they can specify whether they meet their needs sufficiently. Economic calculation also allows for easier investment. If the entrepreneur provides for consumer needs, the involvement of certain factors of production will allow them to achieve profits; otherwise, they will incur losses. Even if entrepreneurs are not discourage with initial losses, they surely cannot incur them indefinitely. The long-term losses cause difficult situation for such entrepreneurs and this should be understood. However, the resulting losses should not be negatively received. Eventually, they are the result of consumer decisions and a signal that rare resources are used in the wrong way — that is, they do not contribute to better satisfying their needs, including these medical (health) services.

However, the budgets of public institutions are not established on the grounds of independent consumer decisions made on the basis of prices and other measures. In this case, speaking about budgets, revenues, or costs is much imprecise. Such institution must distribute available means to specific purposes. It spends funds, but this is not identical to bearing costs under the market conditions. Among other things, due to the artificially stimulated demand, it is very difficult to determine what amount of funds should be directed to individual goals. Public institutions do not have funds (revenues) voluntarily transferred to them by consumers. With their top-down decisions, they must also replace consumers; therefore, above all, they have a problem with determining the correct hierarchy of goals and the scale of the necessary measures. Unhappy consumers cannot resign from paying contributions or propose a higher price for better quality services. Also, decisions regarding investments are becoming problematic. It is not possible to determine the profitability of a given project due to the lack of capability in establishing revenues based on prices (Fuller, 2018). Therefore, obtaining funding for providing access to specific goods and medical services and the investment has little to do with rational targeting of rare resources.

Concept and significance of health in individual and social dimensions

It is very difficult, if not impossible, to achieve an optimal level of goods and medical (health) services which should be provided to individuals to preserve their health. There are at least three reasons for this. First, there is no clear and easily discernible line between health and disease. Second, as a result of the development of medicine and technologies, new and more effective treatment methods, medicines, or medical equipment increase the amount and quality of goods and medical services (health services) and increase choice. Third, for an individual health does not have to be the most important thing. Therefore, a person takes decisions, resulting in a more or less intended use of rare funds for medical (health) services. Under market conditions, this has implications, among other things, for the formation and development of relations between consumer (patient) and physician. The patient knows their body better than the doctor. In turn, the physician has much greater medical knowledge about the patient. There is a specific relationship between them whereby the patient better understands the doctor's recommendations. Because of this, the patient return to health and work more quickly. In this case, the encouragement of adequate trust in the doctor is of special importance, and it also takes time. Building trust is so important, because the patient shares with the physician their personal information. But this is necessary knowledge for the doctor to choose effective treatment methods. In principle, each case is unique due to the fact that people differ in terms of their physiological or psychological makeup. It should also be emphasized that one of the basic conditions for the creation of trust and, subsequently, an appropriate relationship is the voluntary nature of contracts.

These conditions look completely different in a universal health system, which is a system built upon coercion. As indicated by Hayek (1978, p. 300):

> There are so many serious problems raised by the nationalization of medicine that we cannot mention even all the more important ones. But there is one the gravity of which the public has scarcely yet perceived and which is likely to be of the greatest importance. This is the inevitable transformation of doctors, who have been members of a free profession primarily responsible to their patients, into paid servants of the state, officials who are necessarily subject to instruction by authority and who must be released from the duty of secrecy so far as authority is concerned. The most dangerous aspect of the new development may well prove to be that, at a time when the increase in medical knowledge tends to confer more and more power over the minds of men to those who possess it, they should be made dependent on a unified organization under single direction and be guided by the same reasons of state that generally govern policy. A system that gives the indispensable helper of the individual, who is at the same time an agent of the state, an insight into the other's most intimate concerns and creates conditions in which he must reveal this knowledge to a superior and use it for the purposes determined by authority opens frightening prospects.

Under the market conditions, the patient is free to dispose of their funds and with appropriate doctors' recommendations, allocating them the necessary goods and medical services. Doctors' profit depends on customer satisfaction. Meanwhile, in the case of a universal health system, the doctor is obliged to comply with the guidelines imposed on them and faces the problem of permanent shortage of funds and medical services. Additional problems occur when they have to resolve which patients should first be directed to examination or treatment: working people (i.e., those paying premiums) or people who in the post-production age. From the perspective of a public payer, the first group finances the budget (Fund) and the second is only a recipient of collected funds (i.e. do not supply the budget with its own funds). The second group expects adequate treatment, among other reasons because they had also paid premiums before. However, the number of contributions was not related to their former health and present needs. Also, the first group waits for access to medical goods and services. In the market health system, both groups and individual persons may take action to secure their health in ways that do not interfere with the interests of other people. On the other hand, in a universal health system, there are inevitable problems with the distribution of funds between its participants, which may lead to social conflicts. The second group is in a less favourable situation, in the sense that the medical (health) needs of its members are much greater and its economic contribution to financing this system remains negligible. Another problem is the phenomenon of aging societies.

Therefore, the governments are trying to solve this problem through various forms of limiting access to goods and medical services, which comes down to an arbitrary decision what health conditions should be insured in the first place. From this perspective, more arguments might favour focusing on those of working age, because this group can recover faster and pay for contributions. Such people can be easier restored to health than the elderly. In addition, public institutions (e.g., hospitals) can follow their own interest during the treatment process of patients deviating from market conditions. This may be expressed, for example, in an artificial extension of the patient's residence in the hospital, because it gives the hospital additional influences from the Fund. Another example is the pressure on shortening the hospital time for patients requiring a longer stay due to their relatively high costs. In this situation, it is not entirely clear whether the patient is discharged only and exclusively from medical premises. Naturally, market solutions do not consist in the treatment of patients regardless of costs. However, they allow for the effective adaptation of needed and scarce goods to demand (through the price system), thanks to which individual members of society can better understand the situation and take appropriate actions.

Notes

1　Alternatively, also for minimal intervention.
2　This definition is based on the terminology of intervention used by Rothbard.
3　At the same time, changes in other parts of the economy affecting the universal or market health system cannot be ignored.
4　It is also worth noting that economists had already drawn attention to the problem of opportunity costs much earlier. For more on this, see: Bastiat (2010); Sumner (2009).
5　You can also ask the question: if the state knows better than entrepreneurs what the consumer and producers need, why not become an entrepreneur itself?
6　For example, people in post-working age.
7　On the other hand, an example of an attempt to translate market solutions into the public system is the obligation to bear some of the costs directly by the insured, which, in a sense, confirms the usefulness of market solutions by the rulers.
8　From the point of view of governments, they could be referred to as market based.
9　The level of spending on healthcare remains the same.

References

Bastiat F., 2010, *That which is seen, and that which is not seen: An economic essay*, USA: WLC.

Folland S., Goodman A. C., Stano M., 2012, *The economics of health and health care*, USA: Routledge.

Fuller E. W., 2018, Socialized medicine: An accounting perspective, https://mises.org/wire/scocialized-medicine-accounting-perspective (accessed: 13. 09. 2018).

Gorajek M., 2013, Rynek prywatnych usług medycznych w Polsce i na świecie [Private medical services market in Poland and in the world], in Z. Guzel, D. M. Fal, A. Lipka (eds.), *Medycyna ubezpieczeniowa: Underwritinig. Orzecznictwo. Ubezpieczenia zdrowotne* [Insurance medicine – underwriting, certification, health insurance], Warsaw: Poltext.

Hayek F. A., 1978, *The constitution of liberty*, USA: University of Chicago Press.

Hazlitt H., 2008, *Economics in one lesson*, Auburn: Ludwig von Mises Institute.

Sumner W. G., 2009, *The forgotten man*, USA: Sparks Media.

Summary

Increasing the role of the market in the provision and financing of medical goods and services requires not only appropriate institutional solutions limiting the influence of the state. In the first place, the path to such changes must have solid support on the basis of economic theory. That is why creating a theoretical basis for the functioning of a completely market-based health system is so important.

Private health insurance is often presented as a viable alternative to insurance or the public system. At the same time, it is pointed out that such insurance has a number of disadvantages that effectively limit universal financing of access to medical services. In the market system, many people could not take out insurance and would, in a way, be forced to incur significant direct expenses.

However, this presentation of the matter overlooks many important aspects of the market system. The insurance institution is not intended to guarantee universal access to such benefits for everyone. It may cover persons representing the risk accepted by the insurer. Thanks to this, part of the society can free themselves from the problem of relatively high expenses in the future.

However, market solutions are not limited to offering health insurance only. As in most markets, many transactions are done using direct payments. Therefore, the problem lies not so much in the insurance or direct payments themselves as in the regulations limiting the supply and appropriate competition between suppliers. In fact, for example, when making everyday purchases, we do not use 'food insurance'. Although direct payments dominate in such transactions, consumers are not struggling with shortages of food and other goods or services.

Therefore, one of the most effective ways to ensure adequate access to medical services is, inter alia, deregulation of the medical professions and the pharmaceutical industry or greater trust in private institutions that guard the quality. In this case, market processes lead to the

DOI: 10.4324/9781003258957-9

free formation of a rational structure of financing the structure of access to medical services with a significant (and non-conflicting) role of both insurance and direct payments.

It is important because a better understanding of the principles of operation of market solutions increases the chances of their more and more courageous implementation in individual countries.

Moreover, it is not only theory that speaks of the legitimacy of applying market solutions. At the turn of the 19th and 20th centuries, before the emergence of public health systems, there were many market solutions in this area. These were, for example, the so-called fraternal associations – voluntary mutual aid organizations, especially popular with the working class. As late as 1920, more than 25% of American adults were members of such organizations, and the proportion was even higher in the UK and Australia. Such organizations were financed from the monthly or annual contributions of their members, and in return, when necessary, the accumulated funds were transferred to meet individual needs (e.g. financing a doctor's visit). However, over time, a well-functioning market has become the subject of state interventions.[1]

It is worth remembering, especially in times of large and problematic public systems.

Note

1 For more on this subject, see, among others: Long (no date); Harris (2015).

References

Harris B. (ed.), 2015, *Welfare and old age in Europe and North America: The development of social insurance*, London, New York: Routledge.

Long R. T., no date, How government solved the health care crisis, http://freenation.org/a/f12l3.html (accessed: 10. 03. 2021).

Index

Printed in the United States
by Baker & Taylor Publisher Services

Printed in the United States
by Baker & Taylor Publisher Services